An Introduction to Early Childhood

A Multidisciplinary Approach

Edited by Tim Waller

P·C·P

Paul Chapman
Publishing

Paul Chapman Publishing
A SAGE Publications Company
1 Oliver's Yard
55 City Road
London EC1Y 1SP

SAGE Publications Inc
2455 Teller Road
Thousand Oaks, California 91320

SAGE Publications India Pvt Ltd
B1/I 1 Mohan Cooperative Industrial Area
Mathura Road, New Delhi 110 044
India

SAGE Publications Asia-Pacific Pte Ltd
33 Pekin Street #02-01
Far East Square
Singapore 048763

Library of Congress Control Number: 2005923485

A catalogue record for this book is available from the British Library

ISBN: 978-1-4129-1035-4 (hbk)
ISBN: 978-1-4129-1036-1 (pbk)

Typeset by Pantek Arts Ltd, Maidstone, Kent
Printed on paper from sustainable resources
Printed in Great Britain by Athenaeum Press Ltd, Gateshead, Tyne & Wear

Contents

Acknowledgements   vii
About the authors   ix
Verse epigraph   xii
Introduction   xiii

Chapter One
Children's rights to participation   1
Gill Handley

Chapter Two
Protecting children   13
Celia Doyle

Chapter Three
Inclusive practice for children with special
educational needs   27
Chris Hickman and Kyffin Jones

Chapter Four
Joined up thinking in practice: an exploration of
professional collaboration   39
Eunice Lumsden

Chapter Five
Modern childhood: contemporary theories and
children's lives   55
Tim Waller

Chapter Six
Child health   70
Sharon Smith and Tania Morris

Chapter Seven
Children's learning   84
Tim Waller and Ros Swann

Chapter Eight
Studying children   106
Jane Murray

Chapter Nine
International perspectives   123
Tim Waller

Bibliography   144
Index   168

Acknowledgements

The editor would like to acknowledge the contribution of all the authors, who completed their chapters for this book in addition to their 'normal' teaching and work commitments. Colleagues at University College Northampton and Swansea University have been particularly supportive during the period of writing this book and thanks also go to our publisher Jude Bowen for her assistance.

On a personal level, I am very grateful to Peter Silcock, Ian Grosvenor and Dave Hill for their encouragement over a number of years and to my family Janet, Rachel, Amy and Jack for giving me the time and space to complete this project.

Tim Waller
Swansea
June 2005

This book is dedicated to our children

About the authors

Celia Doyle has worked in the field of child welfare, especially child protection, for over 30 years. She was a social worker for local authorities and the NSPCC until her own young family expanded significantly. She then worked independently and entered higher education as a lecturer in social work. Having bachelor's and master's degrees in psychology she also teaches child development. She has continued to research issues relating to child welfare, especially the relevance of the Stockholm syndrome. Her PhD thesis was on the emotional abuse of children. She was later awarded a British Academy grant for research into the role of social support for children who are emotionally abused by their carers. She has published extensively on topics related to child protection with several books on the topic. Currently she is working on a third edition of her 'Working with Abused Children'.

Kyffin Jones is a Senior Lecturer in the School of Education at University College Northampton. He teaches on a range of undergraduate and continuing professional development courses with a primary focus on inclusive educational practices. He is early years trained and has taught in both mainstream and special schools in both the UK and USA. Prior to teaching he worked in adult SEN provision and has recently worked as an LEA advisory teacher for learning and autism. His research interests include effective models for the use of support staff and interactive techniques for pupils with autistic spectrum disorder.

Gill Handley is a part-time lecturer on the BA (Hons) Early Childhood Studies at University College Northampton as well as an associate lecturer for the Open University on the Diploma in Social Work Course. She also works as a Family Court Adviser for The Children and Family Court Advisory and Support Service representing the interests of children in Court Proceedings. She has worked as a social worker in Local Authorities as well as a mentor and supervisor for post-qualifying awards in social work. Her research interests include adoption and post-adoption support as well as children's rights, particularly their rights in relation to court decisions about their future care and contact with family members.

Christine Hickman is a Senior Lecturer in the School of Education at University College Northampton. She teaches on a variety of courses within the school and is a member of the Centre for Special Needs Education and Research. Her particular specialism is autistic spectrum disorders. She has taught in both mainstream and special schools and has worked as an LEA adviser. Her research interests include the correlation between language abilities and challenging behaviour, interactive approaches with children with autistic spectrum disorders and the legacy of the eugenics programmes in Scandinavia.

Eunice Lumsden is the Course Leader for the BA (Hons) Early Childhood Studies at University College Northampton. She also lectures on the Child Care Award in Social Work and an MSC in Child and Adolescent Mental Health and is an Associate Lecturer for the Open University. Prior to joining the team she had over 20 years' experience as a social work practitioner in the statutory and voluntary sector and is a Practice Teacher in Social Work. Her research interests include issues in relation to adoption and the impact of undergraduate study on mature students. She is currently undertaking research into adoption consultative groups.

Tania Morris trained as a Registered Mental Nurse in the 1980s and since has worked as a mental health nurse in a variety of clinical setting. In recent years Tania has been working in the field of child and adolescent psychiatry with her most recent clinical post being Clinical Nurse Specialist working with children with eating disorders. Tania's areas of special interest are eating disorders and child obesity. She is presently a senior lecturer on the pre-registration and post-registration nursing programmes at University College Northampton.

Jane Murray worked as a teaching practitioner in primary and early years' education in the UK for 20 years before moving to her current position as Senior Lecturer in Early Years and English Education at University College, Northampton. She has a particular interest in issues related to children starting school.

Sharon Smith is a Senior Lecturer in Child Health and Community Nursing at University College, Northampton. She is a Registered Nurse and Health Visitor and gained an MA in Med Sci (Primary Health Care) at Nottingham University. Her current teaching responsibilities include coordinating Community Nursing and Early Childhood Studies modules and teaching community nursing and child health across pre- and post-registration nursing courses. In addition, Sharon has a PGCE in primary education and is a governor of a local primary school.

Ros Swann is a Senior Lecturer in Early Years Education at the University of Gloucester. She was formerly the Course Leader of the Early Childhood Studies degree at University College Northampton. She teaches on both the Early Childhood Studies degree and the BA (Hons) degree in Education with QTS. Formerly an early years teacher in Bristol she has also taught in Canadian and American schools. Prior to taking up her post at University College Northampton she taught at the University of Gloucester for 10 years on undergraduate and post-graduate courses. In addition Ros has taught on initial teacher education courses in the USA, Australia, Canada and Finland. Her research interests include the professional identities of early years teachers and the impact of Early Childhood Studies degrees on the training of Foundation Stage teachers.

Tim Waller is Director of Postgraduate Studies in the Department of Childhood Studies at Swansea University. He was formerly Early Years Research Group Leader in the School of Education at University College Northampton and course leader for the BA (Hons) Early Childhood Studies. He taught in nursery, infant and primary schools in London and has also worked in the USA. His research interests include early literacy and ICT, outdoor learning and equality. He has been investigating the use of computers by young children for over eight years and completed his doctoral thesis on scaffolding young children's learning and ICT. His most recent publications concern the application of ICT in the teaching and learning of literacy and he is also involved in an international research project comparing young children's computer use at home and school, in Sweden and the UK and a study designed to investigate the promotion of children's well-being through outdoor play.

Mother always said
    sing child sing
    make a song
    and sing
    beat out your own rhythms
    the rhythms of your life
    but make the song soulful
    and make life
    sing

Micere Githae Mugo

Introduction

Tim Waller

Early childhood (usually described as the period from birth to eight years of age) is currently receiving a great deal of attention, both internationally and in the UK. Since 1997, the Labour government in the UK has invested significant funding in the National Childcare Strategy and the Sure Start programme aimed at supporting families with young children, particularly in areas of economic deprivation. The recent Children Act (2004) proposing the establishment of multidisciplinary children's centres puts integrated services at the heart of early years policy and provision over the next 10 years.

Despite these welcomed initiatives, there is still concern and debate about the availability, cost and quality of care and education for young children, provision for under children three, local involvement and control of childcare and achieving a balance between the needs of children and the needs of parents.

Early childhood is also an emerging area of study. As a result many universities and colleges of higher education in the UK are offering degrees in Early Childhood Studies (ECS) and the number of ECS degree courses has increased significantly over the last four years. Students of early childhood are fortunate in that they are able to draw on perspectives from a number of disciplines, including for example, anthropology, biology, education, health, history, psychology and sociology. On a practical level, books on these subjects are usually placed in different locations in libraries and as the wealth of literature on early childhood grows the field would benefit from a classification of its own.

Much of the recent literature concerning early childhood has contested traditional perspectives of childhood, in particular it has been critical of the central role of 'child development' in explaining children's lives (see Penn, 2005, for example). One of the reasons conventional views of childhood are problematic, is that they relate to a particular type of childhood that is presented as universal for all children. Also, many past studies have not considered the child's perspective. The authors of this book are therefore concerned not to promote an exclusive, western view of childhood that mainly relates to economically advantaged children in wealthy parts of the world such as western Europe, the USA, Canada, Australia and New Zealand.

This book was written as a result of working with ECS students since 1999. A significant number of these students are experienced early years practitioners, most are highly motivated to learn about early childhood and collectively their commitment and achievement have been an inspiration to the authors of this book. All the authors are themselves experienced early years practitioners in the field of education, or health, or social care. The multidisciplinary theme of the book is reflected in their collective understanding of working with young children and their families, and of teaching at undergraduate and postgraduate level. The book also introduces readers to the possibility of multiple, but complementary perspectives on the study of early childhood.

THE AIM OF THE BOOK

The purpose of the book is to provide a contemporary, holistic and multidisciplinary early years reader which covers the theoretical background relating to significant aspects of current international debate regarding early childhood. The book is based partly on the popular curriculum for the Early Childhood Studies degree at University College Northampton. While the aim is to introduce students to some of the key areas, it is also hoped that the ideas presented will challenge student's thinking and encourage reflection, further reading and study. Through a consideration of multidisciplinary perspectives the book is intended as a complement to other recent texts in the field – although, inevitably, it has not been possible to give attention to all aspects of modern childhood and the chapters in this book refer to a selection of possible topics, drawing on the strengths and interests of the authors.

CONTENT

The content is designed for a broad range of readers, in particular those with little previous opportunity to study early childhood. The introductory coverage and emphasis on core ideas make it an appropriate text for students who are new to the field and also students wishing to develop their understanding of contemporary issues in the early years.

The following themes underpin and frame discussion in each of the chapters:

- respecting and protecting children's rights and individuality
- equality of opportunity
- family and community experience and support
- multiprofessional and multidisciplinary collaboration
- opportunities for reflection on the reader's own experience and learning.

The book begins with a consideration of children's rights. Chapter 1 outlines the impact of recent legislation, including the United Nations Convention of Rights of Children (UNCRC) and the Children Act (1989) and the Children Act (2004). The chapter discusses the difficulty of defining children's rights and draws attention to the fundamental conflict between participation rights and protection rights. The final part of the chapter reviews the implications for early years practice in relation to children's participation and examines how children's rights to participation might be advanced.

The focus of Chapter 2 is on protecting children. Readers should be aware that they may find some of the material in this section of the book emotionally demanding. The chapter provides an introduction to some of the key concepts involved in child protection, considering children who might be subjected to a range of abuse and neglect. The main emphasis of the chapter is on abuse by people who are responsible for the care of the children, particularly parents. An appreciation of the obstacles to recognition is given and the impact of abuse on victims is outlined with particular reference to the 'Stockholm syndrome' which results in children showing loyalty and affection for their abusers.

Chapter 3 introduces readers to inclusive perspectives in early childhood. In particular, this chapter includes an overview of the theory involving children with special educational needs in the early years. The definition and philosophy of inclusion is considered within an analysis of the historical and legislative context. The main focus of the chapter is on educational perspectives, although the importance of a multiagency approach is acknowledged. The chapter refers to a number of case studies to illustrate a range of provision for a range of need and outlines a framework for effective practice.

Chapter 4 examines the development of interagency collaboration and the reasons why working outside professional boundaries still remains problematic. The chapter intends to provide the reader with a greater understanding of professional collaboration by clarifying the language of working together; who is and should be involved in collaboration and the ingredients of effective communication. It also considers the role of initial training for early years practitioners in developing the key skills required by professionals working under the agenda current legislation and policy such as 'Every Child Matters: Change for Children' (Department for Education and Skills, 2004e).

Chapter 5 provides an overview of current international literature and research which underpins the study of early childhood. Much of the recent literature has been critical of the central role of 'child development' in theory concerning young children. In order to provide a contemporary account of the young child, Chapter 5 identifies and critically discusses five key tenets of modern theory.

The state of child health in the UK is discussed in Chapter 6 which takes a holistic view of child health and consequently explores children's physical, emotional and mental well-being. The chapter outlines relevant social policy and socio-economic influences are considered including the recent National Service Framework (2004) for Children. Case studies and practice examples are used throughout to illustrate implementation of health programmes.

The focus in Chapter 7 is on how children learn. The chapter opens with a brief overview of traditional theories of learning and then considers learning relationships and dispositions in detail. In particular, the chapter discusses how children's play and sensitive adult interaction and 'scaffolding' can contribute to successful learning. This chapter also provides a synopsis of recent theories of learning including the work of Carr, Rogoff and Vygotsky. The chapter concludes with a summary of the characteristics of successful learners.

Chapter 8 provides an overview of theory and methods of studying children. The chapter begins by examining the contexts and rationale for the study of children in contemporary western society. It explores four major components of the study of children (observation, dialogue, agency and making professional judgements). The chapter continues with exploration and discussion of the domains in which children are studied; the construction of childhood, in the context of the study of children; child study by health care, social care and education practitioners.

The final chapter of the book, Chapter 9, concerns international perspectives of early childhood. The chapter discusses a range of findings from recent international comparisons of early childhood education and care. A number of significant similarities and trends are identified. However, it is recognized that wider evidence is needed to represent a world view of early childhood education and care. The chapter provides an overview of early years policy and provision, commenting in more detail on diverse curricula and notions of 'quality'. Two examples of internationally renowned approaches to early years provision (Reggio Emilia in Italy and Te Whãriki from New Zealand) are briefly summarized to introduce students to the critical insights that can be developed through comparison. The chapter concludes with a consideration of the notion that 'children's services' should be replaced by 'children's spaces' (Moss and Petrie, 2002).

HOW THE BOOK IS ORGANIZED

Each chapter is intended to provide a detailed review of current literature and research. The chapters begin and end with a concise summary and conclude with the identification of further reading and key points for reflection to promote critical thinking about early childhood. Where appropriate, some chapters make use of vignettes, case studies and cameos to illustrate theory and conceptual issues.

Welcome to the study of early childhood!

Chapter 1

Children's rights to participation

Gill Handley

This chapter begins by discussing the difficulties of defining children's rights. There is an assessment of the fundamental conflict between participation rights and protection rights and an evaluation of participation rights under the UNCRC, the Children Act 1989 and the Children Act 2004. The role of competence in the exercise of children's participation rights, and the problems of judging competence are discussed. Conclusions are drawn about the implications for early years work in relation to children's participation and how children's rights to participation might be advanced. Significant questions and suggested texts for further study are given.

The main focus of this chapter will be on the participation rights of children and assessing how much legislation and practice uphold these rights, both in England and internationally. A major argument will be that the participation rights of children are the most difficult and controversial children's rights to be implemented and upheld and are the most likely to be inadequately addressed because of the fundamental conflict between them and the competing rights to protection (Burr, 2004). It will be argued that the latter continue to take precedence as they fit with the predominant discourses of childhood, which see children as in need of guidance, protection and adult control. A major challenge for all those who work with children and young people is how to redress this balance.

WHAT ARE CHILDREN'S RIGHTS?

The language used in relation to children's rights, and rights in general, is confused and confusing. What is understood by the term 'rights' is not a given but reflects different and changing social and political ideologies and values (Roche, 2001). Take, for example, the current notions of individualistic human rights as defined in the European Convention on Human Rights (ECHRC) and the UNCRC. These are rooted in western philosophy and thought, rather than southern or eastern philosophies, as the latter tend to place greater emphasis on family and community responsibilities than on individual interests (Burr, 2002).

The term 'rights' is also used to refer to both moral and legal rights, as well as interests, or notions of what ought to happen in everyday life (Macormick, 1982; Eekelaar, 1992; Freeman, 1983; Fortin, 2003). Although the notion of rights generally involves some idea of an entitlement to something, what the entitlement is to, and who is entitled, again varies and changes with different historical, social and political contexts. For example, women in the United Kingdom were not seen as having a right to vote until the early twentieth century and children were not seen as being a group of people eligible to have rights independently from adults until the latter part of the twentieth century; there is still debate as to whether or not children can be full holders of rights at all, if a precondition is seen as the capacity to be able to choose whether or not to exercise them (Freeman, 1983; Fortin, 2003).

There is the difficulty of defining what is meant by both childhood and its corollary, 'a child'. It is widely accepted that childhood itself is a social construct rather than a biological given (Stainton Rogers, 1989; Franklin, 2002; Jenks, 2004). What is seen as childhood, at what age it starts and at what age it ends, varies and changes (Aries 1962; Fortin, 2003) and there may be different and competing constructions of childhood prevalent at the same time. For example, currently in England, children are seen either as innocent angels in need of protection or as 'villains' in need of control (Goldson, 2001; Franklin, 2002). Burr (2002) argues that street children in Vietnam are similarly seen as either victims or villains. Legislation also constructs childhood and 'the child' in different ways (James and James, 1999). For example, the age of criminal responsibility varies across European legislation from 8 in Scotland, 10 in England to 18 in Belgium. In English law a child is sometimes seen as being a person under 16 and sometimes under 18. For example, a 17-year-old can buy cigarettes but not alcohol; a 16-year-old can work full time but cannot hold a tenancy (see Chapter 5 for a more detailed discussion of childhood).

PROTECTION RIGHTS VERSUS PARTICIPATION RIGHTS

Over the last 30 years, acceptance has grown, in social and political arenas, that children have their own individual rights (Lansdown, 2001). Children are increasingly regarded as agents within their own lives. Rather than seeing children as passive recipients of adults' care and decision-making, children are increasingly being seen as competent to make a range of decisions about themselves (Alderson, 2005; James and James, 1999; Munby, 2004). It becomes increasingly important to acknowledge this competence when the damaging effect of adults' decisions in the past is recognised. For example, children suffered emotional trauma by adults deciding that they should be separated from their parents by evacuation or when undergoing hospital treatment (Lansdown, 2001). Ideas of prescribed and incremental development, which medical and psychological theories have put forward, have been criticised for ignoring the complex and varied range of abilities children of similar ages may have, and for ignoring their individual capacities and competencies (Alderson, 2005) and the different contexts in which they live (Walderkine, 2004). Kaltenborn (2001) found that, in relation to custody and residence disputes, even very young infants could be regarded as having enough emotional intelligence to be able to express reasonable opinions. This is not to say that the overall framework of children developing increasing abilities with age should be dismissed, but rather that a more complex pattern of competencies and abilities should be acknowledged (see Chapter 7).

However, there has continued to be debate and controversy about the extent to which children's rights to protection from various forms of harm and exploitation should take precedence over their rights to self-determination. Child liberationists, such as Holt (1974) and Farson (1974), have argued that children of any age are in need of liberation from the domination and control of adults. Holt (1974) has argued that even very young children should have the right to vote. This view has been challenged by those who consider that children need shielding from the responsibility and burden of making decisions (King, 1987). They see children as fundamentally vulnerable and dependent and therefore in need of protection from various forms of harm and exploitation (James and James, 2004). The extremes of both positions can be challenged, but the differences in the images of childhood, and related perspectives on children's rights that they highlight, do help in understanding the complexity of: 'how to identify children's rights, how to balance one set of rights against another, in the event of conflict between them, and how to mediate between children's rights and those of adults' (Fortin, 2003: 3).

There is also continuing debate about the effectiveness of a rights-based focus per se, in empowering the disadvantaged and vulnerable, which include children. It is argued that rights are abstract legal principles which do not take into account the moral and caring relationships between people (Tronto, 1993 and Heckman, 1995 cited in Roche, 2001). A further criticism of a rights-based perspective is that rights can be given a particular legal construction, which can be disempowering. As James and James (2004: 201) point out, in discussing Dame Elizabeth Butler-Sloss's argument that 'the child [has] a right to a relationship with [his or her] father even if he [or she] did not want it': 'this particular construction of the concept of the child's right has the effect of transforming the child's right into a responsibility or even a duty to see his father, since such a conception of rights fails to endow the child with the equivalent right not to have such contact' (James and James, 2004: 201).

These ongoing debates are reflected throughout legislation and practice in many spheres of children's lives such as health, planning, social work and education, within England, other UK countries and internationally. The next section will now consider some examples of the complexities and conflicts in relation to the exercise of protection and participation rights of children in a number of different contexts.

THE UNITED NATIONS CONVENTION ON THE RIGHTS OF THE CHILD 1989

The UNCRC was adopted by the United Nations in 1989. It was an attempt to improve the living conditions and experiences of children throughout the world. Its aims were to prevent the extreme suffering and exploitation of children, as well as to improve more everyday aspects of children's lives (Alderson, 2005). The 54 Articles of the Convention set out a wide range of rights, which, it argues, all children of the world should enjoy. These rights range from the right to life through to the right to play. Although not incorporated into the law of UK countries, the latter have ratified the UNCRC, as have all other countries in the world except Somalia and the USA. So, potentially, the UNCRC has a worldwide influence on the advancement of children's rights (Burr, 2004).

The UNCRC identifies three types of rights: protection rights, provision rights and, for the first time, participation rights (Alderson, 2005; Franklin, 2001; Burr 2004). The participation rights include the right of children to participate in decisions affecting them (Article 12), the right to freedom of expression (Article 13) and the right to freedom of thought, conscience and religion (Article 14). Although raising the awareness of children's right to participate in various aspects of their lives, the effectiveness and practice of upholding these rights have been limited by various factors.

First, there is no clear definition of what participation means, and how it differs from consultation, involvement or citizenship (Willow et al., 2004). Second, there is no clear explanation as to how participation is to be effected (Crimmens and West, 2004). There have been various models and charts developed to analyse the different extents to which children may be involved in decisions affecting them, and the processes which may be used (Crimmens and West, 2004). These models tend to reflect, in various ways, the fundamental difference between children merely being asked for their views about something and children actually devising decision-making systems themselves (Alderson, 2005; Willow et al., 2004). The various processes involved can be seen as reflecting the difference between seeing children as 'objects' of processes rather than as 'subjects' (Willow et al., 2004), and between seeing children as in need of protection rather than as being agents in their own lives.

Third, the exercise of participation rights under the UNCRC is not absolute. In relation to Article 12, it is dependent on the 'age and maturity of the child', and in relation to Article 14, it has to be consistent with the 'evolving capacities of the child' (UN, 1989). Thus, the level of competence of a child is one of the factors that have to be considered in relation to the exercise of his or her right to participation. How level of competence is to be judged, and who is to judge it, is not clear, but, as later discussions suggest, in practice it will be various groups of adults, not children themselves.

Fourth, there is also evidence that the right to participation tends to be actively overruled when there is seen to be a competing right to protection, as understood under the UNCRC. For example, in relation to street children in Vietnam, aged between 6 and 16, Burr (2002 and 2004) found that the particular view of the rights to protection and education promoted by aid agencies operating within the guidelines of the UNCRC, tended to conflict with what some children said they wanted and what they themselves defined as their needs. Some of the children identified the need to work as significant, as it enabled them to earn money, and thus not be forced to return to rural lives of poverty. By working from a young age, they were also able to give financial support to their families, who could not support them. Some aid agencies sought to protect the children from exploitation, by returning them to more adult-led environments, and by requiring them to receive formal day-time education. By doing so, the agencies failed to listen to the children, understand the contexts of their lives and give credence to the children's own decision to work and be part of the urban communities they saw as their families (Burr 2002, 2004). In Guatemala, similarly, the rights as set out under the UNCRC were found to have little relevance to the everyday lives of children working on the streets (Snodgrass Goday, 1999). Burr (2004) argues that the UNCRC rights are based on a western view of childhood which sees childhood as idyllic. She argues that the assumption that southern and eastern children are seen as in need of rescuing by the more affluent western countries fails to recognize the different needs of children in different social, political and economic contexts. Furthermore, where their needs, for example for income earned on the streets, conflict with the concept of rights to protection, education and family life as promoted by the UNCRC, the latter will predominate, even when children themselves express their own views to have the right to work. Ennew (1995, quoted in Snodgrass Godoy, 1999: 437) points out that, in relation to Guatemalan street children, 'the UNCRC takes as its starting point western modern childhood, which has been globalised first through colonialism and then through the imperialism of aid'. Rather than the UNCRC upholding individual children's rights to participate in major decisions affecting them, these examples show that attempts to impose the UNCRC rights can negate children's participation rights.

THE CHILDREN ACT 1989 AND 2004

The UNCRC provided the context for the enactment of the Children Act 1989, which saw a shift away from children being seen as passive recipients of adult care and control to them being seen as individuals to whom their parents had responsibilities. It also recognized their right to be heard in relation to some decisions affecting them, by having their wishes and feelings taken into account (James and James, 1999).

However, it can be argued that the Children Act 1989 is limited in its support of children's participation rights, in terms of both its principles and its operation in practice (Thomas, 2004; Fortin, 2003). First, children's wishes and feelings are only likely to be considered once the courts become involved in decisions about their care (section 1 [3] [a]). Although there is some limited requirement on local authorities, outside of court proceedings, to consider children's wishes and feelings, (for example, in relation to a child looked after by them (section 22)), there is no general requirement for parents to 'have regard to a child's views when making any major decision affecting them' as there is in Scottish Law (Children [Scotland] Act 1996, section 6[1]).

Second, although the child's welfare is paramount, welfare is seen in terms of protection and safeguarding, not in terms of rights or of promoting active participation (Lansdown, 2001). So, while a court has a duty under section 1(3) (a) to 'have regard to ... the ascertainable wishes and feelings of the child concerned', the court only has to have regard to them, rather than actively consider or act upon them. In contact and residence decisions, they do not have to be considered at all if the parents agree on arrangements for the child (James and James, 2004; Monk, 2004), the assumption being that children's views are irrelevant if parents agree. Furthermore, any weight given to a child's wishes or feelings will depend on their age and understanding; in other words, their level of competence (Monk, 2004).

The recently enacted Children Act 2004 is concerned primarily with the protection of children (Lumsden, this volume). It does not appear significantly to advance the participation rights of children. It could be argued that the establishment of a Children's Commissioner (section 1), who has 'the function of promoting awareness of the views and interests of children' (section 2 [2]), can be seen as a step forward in the advancement of children's rights to participation. However, as with the

Children Act 1989, there is no requirement for any expressed views of children to be actively considered or acted upon. Furthermore, as Hunter (2004) and Goldthorpe (2004) point out, the abilities of the Commissioner to actively advance children's rights in general does not look promising, given that the role has been stripped of its powers to promote and safeguard individual children's rights and has a weaker role in promoting rights than its equivalent in other UK countries.

The widening of the range of circumstances in which Local Authorities must include the wishes and feelings of children (section 53) could also be seen as a positive step forward in relation to children's participation rights. However, under the Children Act 2004, any weight given to them will again depend on the child's age and understanding or competence (section 53 [1] [b] and [3] [b]). So, there is really no significant difference between the two pieces of legislation, despite a gap of 25 years, in terms of the recognition of the rights of children to have an impact on decisions about their lives.

COMPETENCE

There is much confusion within the law as to how the level of competence of a child is to be judged, in what circumstances competence can lead to a child making effective decisions about their lives and in what circumstances their decisions can be overruled. In legal terms, competence is clearly not linked to age. For example, children aged between 16 and 18 are deemed to be sufficiently competent to make decisions in relation to sex and leaving school, but are not considered competent to vote or to marry without their parents' consent. Children aged 10 and over are held to be criminally responsible in English law, and can be made the subject of antisocial behavioural orders under the Criminal Justice Act 1998, but are not deemed to be responsible enough to buy a pet until they are 12 (Fortin, 2003).

The case of *Gillick* v *West Norfolk and Wisbech Area Health Authority* (1985) was seen as a landmark case in terms of young people's rights and in establishing that competence is not necessarily linked to age. It established the principle that a young person under the age of 16 could consent to medical treatment without their parents' consent or knowledge, if they were deemed to be competent enough (BMA, 2001: 34). However, it did not clarify how to assess competence, and again the decision about competence lay in the hands of adults, this time in the hands of a medical practitioner. Moreover, a few years later, the Court of Appeal confused matters by deciding in two cases (Re: R and Re: W cited in BMA, 2001: 35) that the Courts could overrule a teenager's decision to refuse life-saving treatment even when they had been considered 'Gillick Competent'. It seemed that the competence of a child could be overruled depending on the seriousness of the decision involved.

In July 2004, the government introduced new guidance for medical practitioners in relation to young peoples' right to confidentiality about sexual matters and for the first time enabled competent young people to consent to abortion without their parents' knowledge (DOH, 2004). There has been much media-reported criticism of the guidance, particularly in relation to abortion. Mrs Axon, a mother of two teenage girls, has recently been granted the right to a judicial review of the guidance as she disagrees with parents not being routinely consulted in relation to abortion (Powell, 2004). It will be interesting to see if any guidance is given about assessing competence. It will also be interesting to see if the court upholds a young person's right to make their own decision about a major issue such as abortion, or whether their right to protection and their parents' right to be informed, will be seen as more important.

It is interesting to note the support of the government for children's right to make at least some decisions in relation to their health and bodies, in comparison to the lack of support for them to be involved in decisions about their education. As Fortin (2003: 161) states: 'the principles of education law currently show little appreciation for the maturing child's capacity for taking responsibility for his or her school life or for reaching important decisions over his or her education'.

Children have no right to appeal against exclusion from school; it is only their parents who can do that. It is also parents who may be fined and imprisoned if children do not receive adequate education; children themselves cannot make a decision to leave formal education.

This confusion about required levels of competence for participation in decisions can also be seen in relation to contact or residence matters within the courts. In cases where contact is being considered with a parent about whom there have been allegations of domestic violence, the courts have sought the advice of two eminent psychiatrists about the age at which children's views should be taken into account. Sturge and Glazer's (2000: 620) advice is that:

> the older the child the more seriously [their views] should be viewed and the more insulting and discrediting to the child to have them ignored. As a rough rule we would see these as needing to be taken into account at any age; above ten we see these as carrying considerable weight with 6–10 as an intermediate stage and at under 6 as often indistinguishable in many ways from the wishes of the main carer (assuming normal development).

However, it appears from the following studies, that children's views are not routinely sought by courts or professionals involved, and that when they are sought, they may still not be actively heard by the courts.

May and Smart (2004) looked at three County Courts' practices in relation to seeking children's views about contact and residence disputes. In half of the cases they looked at, a CAFCASS (Children and Family Court Advisory and Support Service) officer or a social worker, had been asked to prepare a welfare report, which is expected to include the wishes and feelings of the child as well as advice about the effects of various decisions on the welfare of the child. May and Smart (2004) found that in only half of these cases, thus only a quarter of their total sample, had the children actually been consulted. They found that, of those consulted, children over seven tended to have their views taken seriously, particularly if they could 'vote with their feet' and where there was conflict between the parents. May and Smart were left particularly concerned about the young children involved in disputes, as they appeared to have clear views which were more often overlooked, particularly if they did not accord with the recommendations of the CAFCASS officer, and thus were effectively denied a voice in the proceedings.

James and James (2004) considered how child welfare professionals from CAFCASS represent a child's views to the courts in family proceedings. They included both private law cases, such as contact and residence matters, as well as public law cases where local authorities had sought court orders to protect children from harm. They found that the professional's own understanding and construction of childhood, influenced how they balanced the tensions inherent in wishing to protect the children from the responsibility of making a choice about their future care, whilst also ensuring their wishes were made known to the court. Generally, a more protectionist and welfare perspective dominated and children's voices were filtered out and effectively silenced if they did not fit in with the perspective of the professional involved (James and James, 2004).

It appears from the above studies that family proceedings under the Children Act 1989 are 'more likely to remain a site for upholding contingent and highly romanticized ideas of family life rather than a space for listening and responding to the voices of real children' (Monk, 2004: 166).

SUMMARY

The notion of children having participation rights, what these are and how they can, or should be exercised, is of current and continuing significance for all those who work with children and are concerned about their well-being. In practice, balancing a child's right to protection with their right to participate is difficult for all involved with children. Promoting children's rights to participate does not mean advocating that children should make all decisions themselves, whatever their age or level of competence. However, it is clear that children are not able to participate effectively in many decisions affecting their lives. The influence of dominant constructions of childhood, as well as of prevalent incremental theories of development, can prevent a child's individual needs and levels of competence being recognized, and can lead to him or her being seen as one of a uniform group of people rather than a separate and unique person. As discussed above, this can be seen within the courts making contact and residence decisions in England and within the work of aid agencies working under the auspices of the UNCRC.

It is a difficult challenge for all of us, as adults used to having various amounts of power and control over children, to acknowledge and promote the participation rights of children (Lansdown, 2001). Those working in early years contexts face particular difficulties, as the younger the child the more incompetent he or she tends to be viewed and the less likely he or she is to have their right to participation addressed. However, various methods of facilitating young children's participation are being used in settings as diverse as nurseries and Local Council Planning Departments with encouraging results and significant implications for future practice (see Willow et al., 2004 for a helpful review of various initiatives).

It is incumbent on all of us to recognize the importance of children's active participation in all areas of their lives, not only because it is their right, but also because it can lead to better decisions as well as improving a child's self-esteem and confidence (Thomas, 2001). Children's effective participation will not become a reality unless we are able to actively challenge our own values and beliefs about children as well as those of the many institutions, agencies and organizations which influence children's lives.

QUESTIONS FOR REFLECTION AND DISCUSSION

1. Why is it difficult to define children's rights?
2. Are children's rights, as set out under the UNCRC, universally applicable?
3. Is a rights-based approach helpful in improving the lives of children?
4. How can competence in young children be assessed?
5. How can young children be actively involved in research about their needs?

Recommended reading

BMA, (2001) *Consent, Rights and Choices in Health Care for Children and Young People*. London: BMJ Books.

Fortin, J. (2003) *Children's Rights and the Developing Law*. London: Butterworth.

Franklin, J. (2003) *The New Handbook of Children's Rights: Comparative Policy and Practice*. London: Routledge.

United Nations (1989) *The United Nations Convention on the Rights of the Child*. New York: United Nations.

Useful websites

www.jrf.org.uk (Joseph Rowntree Foundation)

www.article12.com (Article 12)

www.crae.org.uk (Children's Rights Alliance for England)

Chapter 2

Protecting children

Celia Doyle

> This chapter provides an introduction to some of the key concepts that will help early years workers protect children who might be subjected to abuse and neglect. The main emphasis of this chapter is on abuse by people who are responsible for the care of the children, particularly parents. You should be aware that you may find some of the material in this chapter emotionally demanding.

The aim of the chapter is to help early childhood workers gain sufficient understanding of key areas of child protection to enable them to recognize abuse in all its forms. Additionally, an appreciation of the obstacles to recognition is an essential aspect of the chapter. The focus is on recognition rather than policy and procedures. It is important that all people working with children acquire information about what they are required to do in the event of their suspecting or finding that a child is being abused (Calder and Hackett, 2003). They need to be aware of the procedures specific to their profession, position and locality. However, procedures cannot be implemented if a worker fails to recognize that maltreatment is occurring.

In more recent years the case of Victoria Climbé (Laming, 2003) has clearly demonstrated this. Victoria suffered beatings from her aunt who was her main carer and the aunt's boyfriend. They hit her with shoes, football boots, a bicycle chain, a hammer, a coat hanger and a wooden spoon. She was also left naked for long periods, except for a black plastic bag, lying in her own urine and faeces in a bath. She was eventually killed by her aunt and boyfriend. The post-mortem revealed severe burns on her body and 128 injuries. This abuse did not occur overnight. Her suffering was over an extended period, during which she was seen by a number of officials including hospital staff and social workers. All of them failed to recognize the signs of abuse.

Innumerable public inquiries into the deaths of children have shown that recognizing abuse is by no means straightforward (Reder, Duncan and Gray, 1993). However, some knowledge of the underlying dynamics in abuse cases will assist accurate recognition and appropriate implementation of procedures.

WHAT IS ABUSE?

One of the complexities faced by those trying to intervene in abuse cases is that many concepts are 'socially constructed' (Hallet, 1995). This means that different cultures and societies view behaviours very differently. For example, in relation to slavery many past civilizations viewed it as perfectly natural and 'normal' whereas in a large number of modern societies slavery is unacceptable. Similarly, certain types of behaviour towards children, such as denigrating and beating them, is seen as abusive in some cultures, whereas in others tenets such as 'spare the rod and spoil the child' and 'children should be seen and not heard' form the bedrock of child-rearing practices. It is therefore difficult to give precise definitions of 'abuse', however, a key defining feature of child abuse is that there is at least one other person, usually a parent figure, who is misusing the power they have over the child. Hence:

● Physical abuse is the *misuse of physical power* in such a way that it causes physical and emotional harm to the child.

● Neglect is the *failure to use, or misuse of physical and resource power* in such a way that it causes a variety of damage to the child including physical, social, developmental and emotional harm.

● Sexual abuse is the *misuse of sometimes physical but more often superior expert power* (greater knowledge) to coerce and sexually exploit children.

● Emotional abuse is the *misuse of a range of powers* to undermine and damage a child's sense of self-worth.

RECOGNIZING DIVERSITY

Maltreated children will come from a variety of backgrounds representing a range of ethnic groups, religions and cultures. Their families will have varied structures including households with several generations living together or ones with just one adult. Children and their parents will also have a range of abilities and disabilities.

This diversity needs to be acknowledged but it can add to the complexity of intervention because workers have to avoid condemning child care practices that are different but not worse than the mainstream, while not leaving children to be harmed by parenting that is both different and abusive.

WHERE DOES ABUSE OCCUR?

Abuse can occur everywhere, in both private and public arenas, although the more private the arena the greater the risk of abuse. This means that mistreatment is often located in relatively isolated, private families and institutions. There is no one type of family or home in which abuse either always or never occurs. Nonetheless, four groupings of factors point towards increased risks to children. These groupings or contexts – which are not always mutually exclusive – are the unexceptional, chaotic, rigid and deviant ones. These are described briefly below.

Unexceptional context

This is a setting in which children's needs are normally met. Unfortunately, a number of crises and stresses mean that the carer/parent can no longer cope. Sometimes other children in the family continue to be well cared for but, rather like Cinderella, one child is singled out for mistreatment. In other instances all the children are affected.

Case example

A mother with several very young children suffered from severe post-natal depression after the birth of her new baby. Other adults such as her partner and health professionals did not notice that there was a problem. The children became neglected.

Chaotic context

Here there is a general lack of boundaries. The physical and emotional care of the children is erratic. Similarly, discipline is inconsistent with the same behaviours sometimes tolerated and at other times harshly punished depending on the parents' moods. Children are often forced to take on adult roles including parenting the parents or acting as sexual partners. Lack of appropriate boundaries and vigilance means that the children are also exposed to sex offenders' predatory behaviour.

Case example

Jane was six years old and lived with her mother, sister aged three and baby brother of 18 months. No fathers were in evidence although the mother had a constant stream of casual boyfriends. Jane was regularly left to parent the other children while the mother went out socializing. Jane was beaten for offences such as making the gravy too lumpy when she made the family meal, being too tired to manage a large pile of ironing and losing her key when she was meant to let herself in after school.

Rigid context

The care of the children is negative, rigid and punitive. Their parent figures have to be in control at all times and worry about losing 'a grip' on the situation if they do not retain all the power. There is an undercurrent of fear, with the parents terrified of anarchy among their children if they 'give an inch' while the children are scared of their parents' extreme wrath if they make the slightest error. Babies are often subject to strict routines but most difficulties arise once they are toddling. Their parents are intolerant of the mess, defiance and tantrums, which are an inevitable part of toddlers' natural curiosity and increasing independence.

Case example

Mandy aged 7 and her brother aged 4 had, since infancy, been subjected to a very harsh regime by their father. When taken out they would sit for hours without daring to move, speak, eat, drink or go to the toilet. Most people failed to recognize the abuse but instead congratulated the parents on having such remarkably well-behaved children.

Deviant context

Sometimes mimicking any one of the above contexts, here the family system contains one or two people who are seriously damaged and who abuse their power and yet are skilled at exploitation and manipulation. It includes people who are 'addicted' to hospitals and medical care but present their children rather than themselves for treatment.

Case examples

Many of the most extreme examples have made headline news including the cases of Fred West and Rose West (Gloucestershire Area Child Protection Committee, 1995) and Victoria Climbé (Laming, 2003).

UNDERSTANDING AND RECOGNIZING PHYSICAL ABUSE AND NEGLECT

This is not the place to detail all the diagnostic signs of abuse. Even experienced paediatricians and other medical specialists find it difficult to determine the exact cause of many injuries even with the help of sophisticated x-ray and other equipment. However, there are some physical signs of abuse and neglect that can raise a query.

The most obvious are bruises and lesions on the skin of small children. Babies not yet able to roll over or move very far rarely sustain bruising. If they have, then the carers should be able to give a clear explanation that is consistent with the injury. Finger-tip bruising on tiny babies may indicate a carer who is losing control and gripping the child too hard.

When injuries are observed on young children, it is worth asking how they were sustained and whether or not they have been seen by medical staff. To the untrained eye cigarette burns could be mistaken for a skin condition such as impetigo but whether the cause is impetigo or burns, the child needs to be examined by a doctor. Conversely, what sometimes looks like bruising on the back or bottom is really 'Mongolian blue-spot' a harmless birthmark frequently seen on children with a black, Asian or Mediterranean heritage.

Although there are medical or genetic conditions that delay growth, children who are emotionally or physically neglected may also show growth retardation. Non-organic failure to thrive is a diagnosis made when all medical conditions are excluded. It can be confirmed when, in the absence of medical treatment, growth charts show children gaining weight whenever in hospital or care and losing it again after returning home.

UNDERSTANDING AND RECOGNIZING SEXUAL ABUSE

According to Finkelhor (1984) in order for an incident of sexual abuse to occur there has to be:

- someone who wants to sexually abuse a young child
- someone who finds a way of overcoming internal inhibitors (their conscience)

- someone who finds a way of overcoming external inhibitors (for example, protective parents, friends)
- someone who finds a way of overcoming the child victim's resistance (which may be to abuse a child too young to resist effectively).

People who molest young children have a sexual predilection for children independent of their gender orientation (i.e. homosexuality or heterosexuality). If an adult male or female is only sexually attracted to other adults, male or female, then there is very little risk of child sexual abuse. However, some people can only relate sexually to children. Here there is a high risk of abuse and the offenders often fit the typical image of a 'paedophile'. Finally, there are some adults who do not discriminate sexually between adults and children. They pose a considerable risk but may not be so readily recognized as sex offenders, especially if they have adult partners.

Children may also engage in sexual activities with other children. When one child is more powerful than the other either because of age, more knowledge, physical strength or other feature then the activities can become abusive.

The ensuing profile of offenders is based primarily on research into adult male sex offenders. The sexual and offending behaviour of both women and adolescents differs from that of adult males. Despite this, there is reason to believe that female and teenage sex offenders share many of the characteristics described below.

Sex offenders are preoccupied with their own needs and can only see the situation from their own point of view. However, they can sometimes learn to say the 'right' thing. They may appear to be surrounded by family and friends but these relationships are superficial, often exploitative and frequently offenders use them to reassure or attract others. Many have excellent social skills and appear charming and plausible. They frequently collect labels of respectability in order to disarm carers. Nevertheless, there are some offenders who are 'loners' and clearly have difficulties forming relationships with non-vulnerable adults but, conversely, they are very good with children. They know what will attract and disarm a child and can play engagingly with young children.

Sex offenders do not offend as a sudden whim or as a 'one-off'. Their assaults are planned. Collecting child pornography is not a harmless diversion; it is often part of the planning process. They will target a child or group of children. Many will have a preference for a child of a particular gender or type but children outside their target group will still be at risk. Having chosen a victim they will then 'groom' the child. Some offenders use force and threats but most use patience, gently persuading the child to trust them so that the child inadvertently becomes a 'willing' victim. During the assault they will treat the child as an object for their own gratification, sometimes covering the child's face so that they cannot be reminded of their victim's personality. After the assault they will again 'groom' the child, using either threats or persuasion to stop the child telling anyone about the abuse.

Sex offenders have distorted attitudes to children. They believe that even very young children enjoy sexual activities and are ever ready to seduce adults. They will, for example, interpret a small child showing underwear or in tight clothing as 'being provocative' and wanting sex. They also view children as objects designed for adults' sexual pleasure. Often society supports these attitudes, for example, we objectify children and often refer to the child as 'it'.

When confronted with their offending behaviour sex abusers say nothing, make excuses ('I was drunk m'lud') or try to elicit sympathy ('feel sorry for poor me'). Some become threatening, constantly make formal complaints to thwart investigations or denigrate workers using sexist and racist innuendos. Finally, sex offending against children is not a behaviour that can be 'cured'. It can only be controlled, and only controlled with difficulty.

UNDERSTANDING AND RECOGNIZING EMOTIONAL ABUSE

It is often difficult to define emotional abuse but there are two important aspects. First, emotional abuse consists of both acts of commission, for example, verbal abuse, and acts of omission, for example, refusal to praise or encourage a child. Second, there is a misuse of power; parents and other carers exploit their power over the child to actively abuse or fail to use their power so neglect the child's emotional needs. This is illustrated by the following catalogue of emotionally abusive behaviour:

Fear inducing: such as holding a child hostage with a knife to his or her throat or creating insecurity by constantly leaving the child with lots of different 'strange' carers.

Tormenting: includes pretending to break a child's favourite toys or threatening to kill a child's pet.

Degrading: this can be deliberate humiliation, embarrassing a child in front of other people, or denigration and verbal abuse.

Corrupting: consists of using children to carry drugs or taking them on burglaries to climb through small windows. It also includes destructive modelling such as the violent father who encouraged his young son to treat all women with derision and hit his sister and mother.

Rejecting: rejection can be active, such as telling a child she is unwanted, or passive through the avoidance of emotional warmth, praise or cuddles. Closely allied to this is ignoring behaviour, refusing to give the child any attention.

Isolating: may be through locking away in a room or cupboard for very long periods. It can also include preventing a child from socializing or having any friends.

Inappropriate roles: can include being made the scapegoat for all the family's ills, being used as a weapon against the other parent or 'the authorities'. It can also mean being overprotected or infantilized or, alternatively, forced to shoulder too much responsibility.

Emotional abuse can occur outside the family in the form of school bullying or racist taunts by neighbours. It can also be found in every type of family, regardless of race, size, social class or structure. However, children in those families in which there are already a number of stressors are more likely to be emotionally abused (Doyle, 1997).

UNDERSTANDING AND RECOGNIZING CHILDREN'S REACTIONS TO ABUSE

One of the paradoxes encountered in child protection work is that rather than try to escape from the abuse even very young children will hide the signs of mistreatment, refuse to disclose and show a high level of attachment to their abusers. This can be explained partly by the natural feelings of love and attachment that small children develop with their carers in order to ensure survival (Bowlby, 1969). However, this does not fully explain why this attachment is maintained in the face of abuse. It can, nonetheless, be understood if account is taken of the impact of trauma and maltreatment and the psychological process that help people cope with trauma.

The Stockholm syndrome is a recognized range of protective processes with relevance to abused children. The syndrome was first identified when bank employees were held hostage in Stockholm, and it has been observed in hostage, kidnap, concentration camp, domestic violence and other abuse situations. There are a number of stages that victims experience. However, as with grief processes, these stages are not experienced by everyone nor in a clearly defined order.

Frozen fright: when confronted by a situation of terror from which there is no flight or fight possible people 'freeze'. This results in compliance where all the victim's energy is focused on the abuser and is useful because it conserves energy for a time when flight or fight may be possible and compliance is less likely to antagonize the aggressor.

Denial: initial frozen fright gives way to a sense of unreality, 'this isn't happening to me'. This is a useful temporary state which guards against people being overwhelmed by the terror of the situation. But for some victims of abuse this can become an entrenched denial of the severity and pain of the abuse or of the events ever having occurred.

Fear and anger: once reality has sunk in, victims feel fear and anger but it is too dangerous to express these emotions against abusers so victims often project it onto 'outsiders'. Victims believe that they are more likely to survive if their abusers are basically good and care for them, they therefore look for signs of goodness in their abusers and are grateful for any indication of kindness.

Depression: victims also turn their anger against themselves, leading to depression and self-deprecation. They feel useless, worthless and powerless. Having convinced themselves that the abuser is good, they begin to believe that they are being justifiably mistreated because they are bad.

Psychological contrast: the process towards despair or acceptance may be accelerated by psychological contrast, which substantially weakens victims making them more compliant. It is a well known form of interrogation and torture. One person acts as the 'good guy' the other is the 'bad guy'. Alternatively one person behaves in a kindly manner then suddenly becomes threatening and aggressive. In abusive homes one parent may be cruel while the other tries to compensate by being kind. Or, one parent is abusive and then feels guilt so is very kind to the victim – until the next time.

Acceptance: finally, victims of maltreatment reach a state of acceptance. They no longer question the right or wrongs of what is happening to them. Children may appear 'well-adjusted' and their behaviour calm and compliant. They may well have an unquestioning acceptance of the values, justification and behaviour of their abusers.

RECOGNIZING ABUSE AND THE OBSTACLES TO RECOGNITION

There are aspects of a child's appearance, behaviour, development and statements that might be suggestive of abuse. However, recognizing abuse is not straightforward and the final section summarizes the obstacles to recognizing abuse.

Appearance

This includes injuries where there are inconsistent explanations or ones that do not fit with the injury. Neglect might be present if a child is smaller, more poorly clothed or dirtier than most of the children in the family or area. Over-dressed or very loose, swamping clothes may be masking emaciation or injuries. Emotional abuse might be present in a child who appears too clean and smart, especially if he or she is very frightened of making a mess. Finally, there should be concerns when a child shows frozen awareness or appears over anxious.

Behaviour

A child who abuses other children, draws or plays out violent or sexual scenes with peers or toys might be mimicking behaviour they have experienced. Marked changes in behaviour, inability to concentrate and anxiety about going home are always worth exploring, as is rummaging bins or stealing food and comfort items.

Development

Any developmental delay can be an indicator of abuse but equally significant is a sudden regression such as the child whose language acquisition suddenly declines or the previously continent child who becomes incontinent.

Statements

Children may disclose abuse directly, clearly and frankly but others may start to try to disclose indirectly by asking what appears to be a strange or rather personal question. Disclosure sometimes comes through children writing poems or stories; if the child has been sexually abused these may be sexually explicit. Evidently very young children will have difficulty articulating their experiences but children as young as two or three years old have been able to convey aspects of the abuse they have suffered.

WORKERS' ATTITUDES

One of the biggest obstacles to recognition is the professional worker him or herself. Many professionals cannot accept abuse; it is too painful so they ignore the signs or go out of their way to advance more comfortable explanations. They may also convince themselves that parents would never harm their children and the whole discourse of child protection is exaggerated. Other professionals are so emotionally exhausted and burntout that they no longer feel any concern for the child and ignore any potential signs because of the difficulties and challenges it will pose for them.

PROBLEMS RECOGNIZING THE SIGNS

The points below summarize why recognizing child abuse is not always easy. Early years workers need to be aware of the following obstacles to recognition so that they do not make assumptions about the presence or absence of maltreatment:

- Appearance, behaviour and developmental problems can be equally indicative of some other distress or worry.
- Many injuries or skin discolouration can also be indicative of an accident, disease process or birthmark rather than abuse.

- Children with certain disabilities, those for whom English is not their first language and pre-verbal children may not have the vocabulary or communication skills to disclose clearly.

- A 'nice' family can contain an abuser. Some professionals use checklists, which mislead them because although abuse often occurs in identifiable 'risk' situations, it can also occur any time, any where and in any type of family.

- In some cases the abuse is 'victim specific' so that carers/parents who seem to be exemplary in relation to their other children can still abuse one particular victim.

- In sexual abuse cases in particular, the skill of the perpetrator in grooming the victim and their potential protectors into silence is considerable.

- There is the phenomenon of the Stockholm syndrome. Children may appear deeply attached to their parents even when being abused by them.

- Professionals may ignore obvious signs because it is too painful or they are too emotionally exhausted to contemplate the probable suffering of the child.

CASE STUDY

Brook, aged 5 has a sister, Sky aged 8 and a brother, Dale, aged 2. All three children have the same white mother, Ruby. Sky's father was black but was killed in a car accident when Sky was 18 months old. All that is known of Brook's father is that he was a white man and never lived with Ruby. Dale's father is white and is Ruby's current husband.

Since Brook started school a year ago he has been a cause for concern. He is much smaller than the other children in his class. Ruby, her husband, Sky and Dale are all well built. Brook's speech is poor, his development generally delayed and he has difficulty concentrating in class. His clothes are always shabby and he never brings toys from home. Ruby explained that he always breaks his toys and spoils his clothes so that it is not worth buying him new things.

He has frequent bruising to his legs, back and face. His mother says that he is clumsy and often fights with the other children. The staff have noticed his clumsiness in school but he is withdrawn rather than aggressive with both staff and other children. He is afraid of trying anything new in case he makes a mess or a mistake.

CASE STUDY *continued*

When he is asked to draw pictures or talk about home, he always says how much he loves his mother and shows no fear of her.

Is this a clear-cut case of abuse or could there be alternative explanations for all the various points of concern?

What other information – if any – would you need to make firmer or alternative judgements?

Response

There are many indicators of abuse. Brook could be failing to grow, developmentally delayed, fearful of trying anything new and withdrawn because of emotionally abusive behaviour and neglect. The cause of his bruising and generally fearfulness could be physical abuse.

The fact that he does not complain about any maltreatment or seem fearful of Ruby and is attached to her is not an indication that he is not abused. Children may become attached to their abusers, directing their fear onto other people or situations.

Nonetheless, his small stature, clumsiness, developmental delay and quiet anxiousness could simply be innate characteristics. We know little about his genetic inheritance such as the physical size of his father. He may be small because his father was. It would be useful to obtain information about his father if possible.

Although the bruising is suspicious, it could be caused by a combination of falls and bullying by other children. We need to obtain information about the other children and adults in contact with Brook to find out if people other than his parents could be harming him. It is also necessary to exclude any medical condition that might be the cause of his small stature, his clumsiness or a susceptibility to bruising.

Information about his brother and sister could help although if they are well cared for it could be that this is a case where one child is singled out for abuse. Perhaps the mother hated Brook's father and is projecting the hatred onto his offspring. Alternatively, Dale's father may be irritated by the presence of another man's son. It is essential to check that neither parent is known to the police for acts of violence or offences against children.

FINAL COMMENT

Early years practitioners have to balance a fine line between under-reacting by failing to recognize signs, and over-reacting by making assumptions of abuse when there are alternative explanations. The more knowledge and understanding acquired, the easier it is to achieve that balance.

QUESTIONS FOR REFLECTION AND DISCUSSION

1. How are concepts of child protection socially constructed?
2. What are the major obstacles to the recognition of child abuse and neglect?
3. Why is the 'Stockholm syndrome' significant?
4. What are the implications for all early years practitioners of Laming (2003)?
5. How does child protection practice benefit from a multidisciplinary approach?

Recommended reading

Informative introductory works in the field of child abuse include:

Corby, B. (2000) *Child Abuse: Towards a Knowledge Base*, 2nd edn. Buckingham: Open University Press.

Doyle, C. (2005) *Working with Abused Children*, 3rd edn. Basingstoke: Palgrave Macmillan.

Wilson, K. and James, A. (eds) (2002) *The Child Protection Handbook*, 2nd edn. Edinburgh: Harcourt Publishers.

Chapter 3

Inclusive practice for children with Special Educational Needs

Christine Hickman and Kyffin Jones

> This chapter will discuss the issues surrounding the inclusion of children with special educational needs in the early years. Inclusion as a term and philosophy will be defined and discussed within a historical and legislative context. Case studies will be used to demonstrate a range of provision for a range of need. While the importance of a multi-agency approach is commented upon, the main focus is an educational perspective.

'I had a really great time. Nobody talked to me all night!'

Michael (aged 7)

Michael illustrates one of the underlying principles of the education of children with Special Educational Needs (SEN) – the notion that how they see the world and what is important to them is individual and might differ from adults' reality. Michael has Asperger Syndrome which is characterized by impairment in social interaction, and for him an enjoyable night at his local youth club entailed being completely ignored by his peers. This gave him the space to read his favourite science text books uninterrupted. What is clear, however, is that without a firm understanding of Michael's identity both our assumptions and our interventions will not be accurate and might even be detrimental. This chapter will introduce a range of themes relating to the field of SEN while emphasizing the need to adopt a highly individual and sensitive response, one which pays heed to the child's own identity and perspective. While this chapter will recognize that specific disorders and conditions can be linked to general strategies and good practice it will also urge the reader to look more widely than simply labels and categories in order to optimize interventions.

It is true that an understanding of the principles of conditions such as Asperger Syndrome might in some way aid the practitioner, but they are worth nothing without a clear understanding of the individual's perspective. If Michael is to be a fully functioning and included member of society, his inclusion is in some way dependent on our skills to understand him as much as his skills to fit in with us.

Inclusion therefore, is not simply the debate about pupils with SEN being educated in mainstream schools, it is about the role society has in including all children equally.

THE LEGISLATIVE FRAMEWORK

It is clear from the wealth of literature on the subject that the movement towards inclusive education has been part of the educational scene in Britain for many years (Booth and Ainscow, 1998; Drifte, 2001; Dyson and Millward, 2000; Jones, 2004; Norwich, 1997; O'Brien, 2001; Roffey, 2001; Wilson, 1998; Wolfendale, 2000). Some maintain it can be mapped back to the Education Act 1944 which extended the right to education to most (but not all) of Britain's children as Stakes and Hornby (1997: 24) highlight:

> Children with SEN were to be placed in one of eleven categories of handicap: blind, partially sighted, deaf, partially deaf, epileptic, educationally subnormal, maladjusted, physically handicapped, speech defective, delicate and diabetic. The 1944 Act required that LEAs had to ascertain the needs of children in their area for special educational treatment. It indicated that this should be undertaken in mainstream schools wherever possible.

It is important to note that, at this time, disability was firmly categorized into medical subgroups and that the remit of education was to treat rather than educate. Subsequent reports such as that by the Warnock Committee (1978) highlighted the principle of integrating children with disabilities and developed the process of obtaining a statement of special educational need. In effect, a contract between pupil and educational provider based on careful assessment. The findings of Baroness Warnock and her team helped inform the subsequent 1981 Education Act.

A greater emphasis was given to the education of children with special needs during the 1980s and early 1990s and this culminated in the implementation of the Code of Practice for Special Educational Needs in 1994, updated in 2001. At the time, this was the most prescriptive guidance on special needs to have been issued by the UK government. It aimed to expand the roles and responsibilities of schools and local education authorities (LEAs) highlighted in the 1981 Education Act. This trend of redefining SEN provision has continued and during the past decade has gained momentum and evolved considerably. The Code of Practice (2001) stresses that 'provider' means all settings which early years children may attend, therefore adherence to such guidelines impacts upon a wide range of professional practice. The early years have specified strands in the Code: *Early Years Action* and *Early Years Action Plus*. According to Drifte (2001: 4), 'both stages involve individualised ways of working with the child, including the implementation of IEPs (Individual Education Plans), on a gradually increasing level of involvement'.

Early years provision has always crossed over fields, i.e. health and education, therefore previous legislation such as the 1981, 1993 and 1996 Education Acts may not have enabled a more cohesive approach to SEN in the early years (Wolfendale, 2000: 147). However, more recent legislation appears to be addressing this (Roffey, 2001: 14). *Curriculum 2000* contains an inclusive statement concerning the provision of effective learning opportunities for all pupils. It sets out three principles that are essential to developing a more inclusive curriculum:

1 Setting suitable learning challenges.
2 Responding to pupils' diverse learning needs.
3 Overcoming potential barriers to learning and assessment for individuals and groups of pupils (QCA, 2000).

THE GLOBAL AND NATIONAL PERSPECTIVE

Inclusive policies have been found increasingly higher up the agenda of the UK government, local education authorities and individual schools. This is due in some part to the United Nations Educational, Scientific and Cultural Organisation (UNESCO) Salamanca statement on principles, policy and practice in special needs education published in 1994. This statement urged national governments to pursue inclusive educational practices for all children.

It is the consensus of many educationalists (for example, Booth and Ainscow, 1998) that the goal of inclusive education is a worthy one but it leads us to ask two questions. First what do we mean by inclusive education or 'inclusion', and second why do we need it? Finding a concrete definition of inclusion can be difficult and it is clear that confusion abounds, affecting providers, parents and the pupils themselves.

The Centre for Studies on Inclusive Education (CSIE) is an independent educational charity set up in 1982. In their literature they define inclusion as, 'disabled and non-disabled children and young people learning together in ordinary pre-school provision, schools, colleges and universities, with appropriate networks of support' (CSIE, 2000: 1).

Such a short definition belies the incredibly far-reaching, controversial and challenging task of the inclusion movement. Essentially the CSIE is advocating the end of segregated education and with it the traditional model of special education in this country. It follows that there must be a compelling argument behind this radical approach if one is to answer the second of the above questions. Why do we need inclusion? Again the CSIE (2000) answers this in a succinct and direct way, 'Because children – whatever their disability or learning difficulty – have a part to play in society after school, an early start in mainstream playgroups or nursery schools, followed by education in ordinary schools and colleges is the best preparation for an integrated life' (CSIE, 2000: 2).

Early intervention is an essential component to any debate on early years and inclusion (Mortimer, 2002). In this respect the UK government's agenda includes healthy living, community support, multi-agency working and a focus on families. Initiatives such as Education and Health Action Zones and Sure Start are examples of these ideals (Wolfendale, 2000: 149).

INCLUSION: A HUMAN RIGHT?

It is clear therefore that issues of equality and human rights are central to such a rationale, and as the above quote highlights, education is only one part of the picture. The drive towards inclusive education has to be seen in a wider societal context if it is to be meaningful and successful. In other words, inclusion should be less about teachers and pupils and more about the responsibilities of all citizens. As Huskins (1998: 10) makes clear, 'communities have responsibility for providing the social, health and educational services necessary to complement the role of families in promoting the development of the "whole" child and for addressing social inequalities'.

As mentioned previously there has been a need to bring together the differing areas in the field of early years. Inclusion is promoted by careful, joint planning, utilizing a broad range of expertise from a range of professionals in a cohesive manner.

Soon after gaining power in May 1997 the Labour government published the White Paper *Excellence in Schools* in June 1997. This was followed by the Green Paper, *Excellence for all Children* published in September of the same year. These documents highlighted a clear shift in traditional policy towards children with disabilities. The educational landscape has changed considerably since the Education Act of 1944. Merely providing a school place for children with special needs is no longer acceptable; the quality of that education has to be second to none.

MODELS OF DISABILITY AND THE ROLE OF SPECIAL SCHOOLS

If large numbers of children with SEN are in specialist provision, we need to ask why. This has resonance for the very young child with a disability, whose future may seem to be firmly placed in a specialist setting. The answer to this question might lie in the dominant position of the medical model. In this model, the child's needs are defined in medical terms and the idea that these children have different and exclusive needs is perpetuated. Also implicit in the medical model is the notion of impairment and that problems are predominantly found within the child. Inclusion is aided by the use of educational terminology, e.g. 'learning difficulty', rather than reliance on categories ('autistic child') or medical labels. However, there is often a strong desire for a diagnosis and its subsequent 'label' as that is seen to be the route to support and funding for the child. It is here we see the areas of health and education both involved with a child, and where we would aim to see multiagency working and partnership. The Early Years Development and Childcare Partnerships (EYDCP) bring new opportunities for a coming together and joining up of different settings, services, agencies and disciplines (Mortimer, 2002: 47). Hall (1997: 74) describes the causal link between the medical model and segregated specialist education thus:

> The medical model is only able to see the child and his impairments as the problem, with the solution being to adapt the child and his circumstances to the requirements of the world as it is. All of the adjustments must be made to the lifestyle and functionality of the child. Hence a range of prosthetic devices will be offered, along with a separate educational environment and transport to facilitate attendance. The notion that the world might need to change hardly arises because the child *has* and *is* the problem.

The final sentence of the above quote is important and outlines the argument of the Disability Movement, which has gained momentum in both the global and national arena. This argument advocates the use of the social model of disablement. Such a model is concerned with environmental barriers, and the notion that it is these barriers that disable people. The Disability Movement makes it clear that the effective removal of impairments is rare, but a great deal more can be achieved by removing those barriers, which include not only the physical environment, but also associated policies and attitudes.

This sentiment was made law within the provisions of the Special Educational Needs and Disability Act (2001) and this has wide implications for the inclusion of children who were excluded from mainstream institutions for reasons of accessibility. Accessibility mirrors our interpretation of inclusion as a varied and individual concept. What is required is a broadening of the concept of access to include whatever barriers to learning impact on the individual child.

Sainsbury (2000), an adult with autism, is aware of the debates regarding identity, inclusion and disability rights and advocates a wide interpretation of these factors to meet the particular needs of those on the autistic spectrum. This is demonstrated by her definition of access and what constitutes an optimum learning environment for pupils with Asperger Syndrome: 'we don't need ramps or expensive equipment to make a difference for us; all we need is understanding' (Sainsbury, 2000: 9).

Although the social model is now favoured above that of the medical model by many disabled people and their advocates, it is also true that for a great number of educationalists, parents and children the segregated model has a lot of defenders. Jenkinson (1997: 10) categorizes the perceived advantages, which are broken down into practical and economic factors, together with specific effects on disabled and non-disabled children. She highlights the efficiency of necessary aids and equipment, specialist teachers and ancillary

services to be located in one place. This complements the perceived benefits to the students found in smaller classes with more one-to-one attention
and a curriculum pitched at an appropriate level.

It is also fair to say that the majority of professionals in specialist provision feel they are working in the best interests of the children they teach.
In many respects 'special education' is seen as a worthy profession with
established models of good practice and pedagogy. Any suggestion that
they are helping to deny disabled children basic human rights or perpetuating institutional discrimination would be denied by many. A more
cynical observation would be that it is in the interests of the two
branches of education to remain distinctive to preserve the status quo
and consolidate their expertise and influence.

HINDRANCES TO INCLUSION

Current UK government policy seems to be increasing scrutiny of student attainment and performance related indicators with the publication
of school league tables (Gabriel, 2004). To some teachers, inclusion is
perceived as a hindrance to these factors as it is often felt that *in*clusion
is merely the opposite of *ex*clusion. As a result many teachers see the
acceptance of children with emotional and behavioural problems into
their class as synonymous with inclusion and to the detriment of their
mainstream peers.

Social inclusion can therefore cause a great deal of anxiety in schools, as
staff might be reluctant to consider issues of behaviour within the context of special needs: 'Teachers in normal schools may be willing to
accommodate the "ideal" child with special needs in their classroom –
the bright, brave child in a wheelchair – they will still want to be rid of
the actual "average" child with special needs – the dull, disruptive child'
(Tomlinson, 1982: 80).

Fortunately the concept of education for *all* is a right that is enshrined
in law at local, national and international levels. Issues regarding the
inclusion of children with SEN are ongoing and often controversial,
highlighting the evolutionary nature of this debate. However, we must
not lose sight of the fact that in the recent past, many of the children at
the centre of this agenda were deemed ineducable. Scholars must recognize the nature of these advances and place the current arguments into
this wider historical perspective.

Case studies

The following case studies demonstrate the experiences of a range of children in the early years and the varied nature of SEN and support. They show the difficulties facing practitioners involved in setting up appropriate interventions together with an indication of the areas that require targeting.

CASE STUDY

Chantelle is 3 years and 2 months old. Her nursery teacher was concerned about her overall development which appeared to be delayed in all areas. Chantelle's speech is particularly problematic. She is difficult to understand and salivates excessively when speaking, resulting in constant 'dribble' on her chin and chest. Her social behaviour is immature and she is becoming increasingly ostracized by her peers.

This visibly upsets her; staff feel she is becoming more 'naughty' in an attempt to gain favour and attention from the others. However, her nursery teacher's opinion is 'she doesn't help herself ... and she is so smelly, would you want to be friends with her?'

The LEA support service pre-school team became involved as part of 'Early Years Action' (Code of Practice, 2001). Chantelle was tested for developmental verbal dyspraxia. This affects the muscles in the throat which control all movement for speech, and swallowing. She was found to have difficulties in this area as well as general learning difficulties. Staff were given details of a range of exercises to do with Chantelle in order to strengthen and help co-ordinate these muscles.

A referral was also made to the Speech and Language Therapy service. The LEA support service teacher made a number of recommendations. Social inclusion was prioritized on Chantelle's IEP.

The need for an advocate for Chantelle was stressed to the teacher. There were concerns about the standard of care at home but this was clearly not Chantelle's fault. A Support Assistant who primarily worked with another child was particularly sensitive to the situation and she began to include Chantelle in small group activities. Positive modelling of behaviour towards Chantelle from the Assistant began to positively affect the behaviour of her peers. Chantelle was also introduced to a visual timetable using photographs of the day's activities. Photographs were also used to help her make choices, for example, between different play equipment. This had the effect of slowing her speech down and enabling her to focus upon pronunciation.

CASE STUDY

Ashlyn was born prematurely and has a diagnosis of cerebral palsy. She is 18 months old. Her parents were devastated when they were given the diagnosis, and had no idea what the future may hold for them and their daughter.

A referral was made to the local Portage service. This was funded by the LEA. Fortnightly visits were set up by the Portage home visitor, whose background was in physiotherapy. In the first visit Ashlyn was observed and the Portage worker played with her. The Portage checklist was introduced to her parents and they were encouraged to set aside a regular time each day to work with Ashlyn. Written weekly teaching activities were agreed with Ashlyn's parents, based on her priority areas of need. In Ashlyn's case these were gross motor skills, fine motor skills, self-help and communication/socialization. The parents then did daily activities with their daughter. This made them feel totally involved in her progress, and they said they felt their knowledge about Ashlyn's condition was greatly enhanced.

New teaching targets were developed over time; each stage was evaluated taking into account the views of the parents. Ashlyn has made considerable progress. Ashlyn's mother has joined a parent support group which has a toy library. Both parents feel more positive about the years ahead.

CASE STUDY

Shaun is 4 years and 8 months old and attends the nursery department of his local primary school. He is described as an energetic and boisterous child. Staff find him to be happy and sociable, actively seeking contact with peers and adults. Shaun's parents, however, have been worried about him for some time as they feel he is developing at a slower rate than his siblings did. This view is supported by the nursery teacher who has confirmed that Shaun's language is significantly less developed than his peers and he only has a repertoire of a few key words. Shaun also has a problem with understanding and rarely responds to instructions given verbally unless they are broken down into short words and phrases.

Shaun spends a lot of time playing in the water tray and he gets very excited repeating the same kind of activities, often getting wet and pouring water over himself and others. Recently he has become anxious when told to move on to another activity and has, on occasion, demonstrated defiance.

▶

CASE STUDY *continued*

At table-top activities, Shaun enjoys playing with a variety of objects, but has poor fine motor control. He does not seem to notice his difficulties.

He will play alongside peers, but will not attempt to converse with them, or respond to their questions. The family GP has suggested that Shaun might have general learning difficulties. There has been no contact with the authority's Educational Psychologist as yet. Following advice from the GP, staff have started showing Shaun photographs of activities in an attempt to help with transitions. This has been successful.

A variety of photographs have been made available to Shaun, including favourite toys, family and objects. He has started to bring the photograph to an adult and say the associated word, e.g. 'crisps' in an attempt to communicate his wishes.

CASE STUDY

John is 7 years and 10 months old. He has recently been given a diagnosis of autistic spectrum disorder. John attends a large inner city mainstream primary school and has brothers in the school.

John has odd and idiosyncratic speech, which often has a maturity beyond his years, e.g. 'I find this work tedious in the extreme'. Both peers and staff find it difficult to understand what he is saying as he often mumbles or whispers his words and makes little use of eye contact or gesture. He seems to 'switch off' if adults address him directly.

John is an avid reader of books, particularly non-fiction books relating to football statistics. As a consequence of his communication difficulties John is ostracized and bullied by his peers who find him odd.

John has begun to go up to groups of boys at lunchtime and forcefully push them, causing them to chase and abuse him. Staff have repeatedly told him not to, but this has no effect and John gives the impression he enjoys the chase and insists that he is *playing* with the boys.

Recently a volunteer has come in at playtime and has introduced some playground games, some with a football theme. He wrote a simple set of rules to accompany each game for the children to refer to. John was excited to read the rules and became animated when the games were played. He tried to direct his peers, and it was noticeable that they were far more accepting of him in this context.

CASE STUDY *continued*

Staff have followed on from this approach in the classroom and have started to write down information for John to refer to. He has responded well to this and staff have noticed that he is far more willing to communicate with them. They have also made attempts to use his knowledge of football-related statistics to lift his profile within the class. His peers are very impressed with his knowledge, and while they still regard him as odd, they respect his abilities and tolerate his differences.

SUMMARY

These case studies serve to illustrate the notion that there are aspects of good practice that are generic with regard to the support of these children and work across the board. These include:

- the use of structure and routine
- practitioner language
- visual systems
- individualized motivators
- practitioner awareness and knowledge
- appropriate and creative use of support staff
- knowledge of the individual child's perspective and sensibilities
- a recognition of the role of other children and peer relationships
- a recognition of the role of parents
- a commitment to an inclusive philosophy.

It is equally important, however, that strategies are optimized to take account of those individual factors particular to the child. These include the sensitive use of John's football interests and Shaun's highly visual learning style. It is not the purpose of this chapter to provide a 'one size fits all' definition of inclusion, but rather to promote the notion that it is a process which is highly individualized and wider than the issue regarding specialist versus mainstream provision. Effective early years practitioners will be those professionals who are able to look beyond labels, diagnoses and particular settings and look to individual factors to ensure the child with SEN is both prepared for and accepted within society.

ISSUES FOR REFLECTION AND DISCUSSION

1. What are the benefits of early intervention?
2. Consider the current debate regarding the inclusion of pupils with Behavioural Emotional and Social Difficulties (BESD) in mainstream settings. What is your opinion on this aspect of inclusion?
3. How does the legislative framework regarding access issues affect children you know or have worked with?
4. What issues are there in respect of promoting self-advocacy with children who have special educational needs?
5. How should the rights of parents and guardians be taken into account?

Recommended reading

Drifte, C. (2001) *Special Needs in Early Years Settings: A Guide for Practitioners*. London. David Fulton.

Roffey, S. (2001) *Special Needs in the Early Years: Collaboration, Communication and Coordination*. London: David Fulton.

Jones, C. (2004) *Supporting Inclusion in the Early Years*. Maidenhead: Oxford University Press.

Chapter 4

Joined up thinking in practice: an exploration of professional collaboration

Eunice Lumsden

This chapter examines the development of interagency collaboration and the reasons why working outside professional boundaries still remains problematic. The chapter intends to provide the reader with a greater understanding of professional collaboration by clarifying the language of working together; who is and should be involved in collaboration and the ingredients of effective communication. It also considers the role of initial training for early years practitioners in developing the key skills required by professionals working under the current policy agenda of 'Every Child Matters: Change for Children' (Department for Education and Skills, 2004e).

The Children Act 2004 received royal assent on 15 November 2004 and purports to herald a new era of services for children and families. High on the political agenda and enshrined in the legislation is the importance of integrated services and by implication, the need for collaboration between professionals (Children Act, 2004). Therefore this chapter intends to provide the reader with a greater understanding of professional collaboration by clarifying the language of working together; who is and should be involved in collaboration and the ingredients of effective communication. It will also consider how initial training, provided by courses in early childhood, have a role in developing the key skills required by professionals working under the agenda of 'Every Child Matters: Change for Children' (Department for Education and Skills, 2004e).

However, the practice of agencies working together is not a new concept, indeed the government provided guidance for interagency working under the Children Act 1989 and in Working Together Under the

Children Act (Department of Health, 1991). The difference at present 'is the increased emphasis that recent governments have put on joint working' (Harrison et al., 2003: 8). They quote Tony Blair who argues that: 'whether in education, health, social work, crime prevention or the care of children "enabling" government strengthens civil society rather than weakening it, and help families and their communities improve their performance ... New Labour's task is to strengthen the range and quality of such partnerships' (Blair, 1998, cited in Harrison et al., 2003: 8).

Indeed as Butcher (2002: 189) states: 'the collaborative imperative is "at the heart" of the framework for change'. Thus, integrated services are at the heart of the government initiative *Every Child Matters* and the Children Act 2004 provides the legal framework to facilitate the programme of change over the next 10 years.

For students and practitioners in the early years this is an exciting and challenging time as the importance of government policy that involves 'joined up thinking' and collaborative working becomes integral for improved outcomes for all children. Organizations working with children will have a duty to work in partnership and there will be an integrated framework for inspection to ensure that policy becomes reality (Department for Education and Skills, 2004e).

How the government vision will actually be translated into practice is unknown and any research into how this legislation impacts on practice is at an embryonic stage. However, as early years practitioners, you will be instrumental in developing the workforce who will not only develop current practice but also put the evolving policy into practice, especially in relation to the below outcomes that children have identified as being important:

- being healthy
- staying safe
- enjoying and achieving
- making a positive contribution
- achieving economic well-being.
  (Department of Education and Skills, 2004e)

In order to meet this challenge the government has produced the following agenda of change to overhaul and improve the provision for children and their families:

- the improvement and integration of universal services in early years settings, schools and the health service
- more specialised help to promote opportunity, prevent problems and act early and effectively if and when problems arise
- the reconfiguration of servicees around the child and family in one place, for example, children centres, extended schools and the bringing together of professions in multidisciplinary teams
- dedicated and enterprising leadership at all levels of the service; and the development of a shared sense of responsibility across agencies for safeguarding children and protecting them from harm
- listening to children, young people and their families when assessing and planning service provision, as well as in face-to-face delivery (Department of Education and Skills, 2004e).

It is evident from the government initiatives that central to its thinking is the importance of professionals working effectively together for the benefit of children, young people and their families. However, as previously highlighted, the Children Act 1989 had enshrined the importance of partnership working and professionals have historically worked together to provide services and share information (Children Act 1989; Department of Health, 1991; Loxley, 1997). Indeed, The Assessment Framework of Children in Need and their Families (Department of Health, 2002) hoped to enhance the multiprofessional approach and there are many examples of effective interagency initiatives and multidisciplinary teams working in health, education and social care settings. For example, Child and Adolescent Mental Health Services, the Sure Start initiative and centres of excellence, such as Penn Green in Northamptonshire (Carnwell and Buchanan, 2005; Housley, 2003; Leiba, 2003; Lloyd et al., 2001; Pinkerton, 2001; Thompson, 2003; Whalley, 2001). Despite this, one of the common factors identified in child death inquires is the difficulty that professionals have in working together to safeguard children (Lamming, 2003). Indeed it is the death of Victoria Climbé on the 25 February 2000 that has fuelled the current political agenda that is legally requiring effective integrated working (see Chapter 2).

While applauding the vision, if practitioners are to consistently work effectively together, there needs to be an understanding of why this area is problematic and what can be done to develop a greater shared understanding of how we will navigate through the emerging issues.

THE LANGUAGE OF COLLABORATION

Whether just starting out in a career in health, social care or education, or in practice, you will find that the language of collaboration is varied and there is not necessarily a common understanding of what the different terms encompass and who is included in the collaboration process. In practice the terms partnership, collaboration, interagency work and working together are often used interchangeably and different professionals can have different interpretations of what they mean. Therefore, for the purposes of this chapter collaboration will be used as an umbrella term embracing the different terminology in common usage.

Over the last 30 years these terms have evolved to become integral to discussions about how professionals can develop working patterns that meet the complex needs of adults and children and 1973 saw the government specifically addressing collaboration (DHSS, 1973). Since then there have been a series of government publications and legislation embracing issues of partnership between professionals and the involvement of service users (Children Act 2004; Department of Health, 1991, 2000; Loxley, 1997; Sanders, 2004). Initially the focus was on health and social care with child protection procedures being pivotal in the development of collaborative working in relation to children and their families (Calder and Hackett, 2003; Department of Health, 1991; Sanders, 2004). Education has also increasingly become an active player and the importance of collaboration between health, social care and education is central to the government initiative Every Child Matters that underpins the new Children Act 2004. The message is very clear that professionals and those using the services provided need to be working together more effectively.

While this is the current situation there is a lack of clarity over what is meant by the terms. Lloyd and Stead (2001) provide some useful definitions to assist practitioners in their understanding of the language of working together (see Table 4.1). One term missing from their list is partnership, though this term is in frequent use in health, social care and educational settings. Harrison et al. (2003: 4) reviewed the literature on partnership and highlighted 'that there is no single, agreed definition

Table 4.1 Terminology

Interagency working	More than one agency working together in a *planned and informal way*
Joined-up	Deliberate and coordinated planning and working which takes account of different policies and varying agency practices and values. This can refer to thinking or to practice or policy development
Joint working	Professionals from more than one agency working directly together on a project, for example, teachers and social work staff offering joint group work. School-based interagency meetings may involve joint planning which reflects *joined-up* thinking
Multiagency working	More than one agency working with a young person, with a family or on a project (but not necessarily jointly). It may be concurrent, sometimes as a result of joint planning or it may be sequential
Single agency working	Where only one agency is involved may still be the consequence of interagency decision-making and therefore may be part of a joined-up plan
Multiprofessional workings	The working together of staff with different professional backgrounds and training
Interagency communication	Information sharing between agencies – formal or informal, written or oral

Source: Lloyd and Stead (2001)

and that sometimes the term is used interchangeably with the term col-laboration'. They suggest that a more helpful approach is to consider the characteristics of partnerships that are successful:

- Involve more than two agencies or groups, sometimes from more than one sector (private, public, voluntary) and include the key stakeholders – that is, those who are primarily affected by the problem and /or have a responsibility for developing solutions.
- Have common aims, acknowledge the existence of a common problem and have a shared vision of what the outcome should be.
- Have an agreed plan of action or strategy to address the problem concerned.

- Acknowledge and respect the contribution that each of the agencies can bring to the partnership.
- Are flexible in that they seek to accommodate the different values and culture of participating organisation.
- Consult with other relevant parties that are not in the partnership.
- Exchange information and have agreed communication systems.
- Have agreed decision making structures.
- Share resources and skills.
- Involve the taking of risks.
- Establish agreed roles and responsibilities.
- Establish systems of communication between partners and other relevant agencies.
  (Harrison et al (2004:4))

Sanders (2004) also contributes to the language debate by considering the impact of whether inter, multi or trans are used. He states: 'These word parts have different meanings. "Inter" means between, implying the link between the two entities; "multi" means many, and "trans" means across' (Sanders, 2004: 180). He goes on to argue that while multi and inter are most frequently used, multi is preferred because it implies more than two in relation to collaboration. Loxley (1997) draws attention to the fact that the only explicit attempt at identifying what is meant by the term was by the Joint Working Group on collaboration between Family Practitioners committees and District Health Authorities (DHSS, 1984). She discusses their view of collaboration as 'mutual understanding and respect for each other's role and responsibility; identification of areas of common interest and concern; the establishment of common goals, policies and programmes' (Loxley, 1997: 20). Banks (2004) and Whittington (2003) provide useful discussion about this area and discuss a continuum of working together. Banks (2004) introduces the different levels of working together; strategic and team/operational. Whittington (2003: 24) adds a further level of intermediate partnership and collaboration. For him the continuum ranges from less to more integrated services. At one end there are separate services which 'collaborate on an ad hoc basis' and, at the other, Care Trusts which exemplify organized integrated services.

Banks (2004) also cites the work of Carrier and Kendall (1995) in relation to the useful distinction between multiprofessional and interprofessional working. She states: '*multiprofessional* working, where the traditional forms and divisions of professional knowledge and authority are retained ... *interprofessional*, where there is a willingness to share and give up exclusive claims to specialist knowledge if the needs of service users can be better met by members of other professional groups' (Banks, 2004: 127).

As she goes on to argue, many teams are somewhere between these two and the main aim of this approach is a belief in the idea that the service user will receive a better service. While this may be the case, this approach to the delivery of services is not without difficulties, as professionals with different values, cultures, ideologies and professional identities come together (Calder, 2003; Loxley, 1997; Banks, 2004). Indeed research into this area (Banks, 2004: 134) has highlighted that some of the difficulties in professional working together 'are around the incompatibility of the managerial structures, procedures and systems operating in the parent agencies employing the practitioners'. Calder and Hackett (2004: 10) adds to this debate and includes factors such as different 'background and training'; 'varied attitudes to family life'; 'stereotypes and prejudices' and 'communication'. The debate becomes more complex when we consider the balance of power between the professionals involved in the collaboration and how this impacts on services being provided. For example, how can different professionals come together and work effectively on the same case when there is a lack of parity in pay scales, work conditions and context. However, there is another layer and one which is arguably the most important in service delivery, that is the diverse needs of the community for whom the services are provided (Leiba and Weinstein, 2003; Loxley, 1997).

Working together therefore is a complex area bringing together not only the needs, experience and professional identities of those involved but also the complex needs of those requiring services. As Loxley (1997: 49) states: 'If collaboration is to be a reality and not a myth, these differences need to be identified and acknowledged at all levels, so that they may be honestly faced and taken into account when assessing whether collaboration is feasible, and/or the most effective or efficient response.'

Accepting that there is not a definition that encapsulates all the complexities of collaboration indicates that there may be a case to simplify language associated with working together in order to provide a shared foundation on which to build our knowledge and working practice. Those working with children and their families and those engaging in early childhood studies not only need to have a shared understanding about the different terminology in use (see Table 4.1) but also an understanding of the ingredients of effective collaboration; the range and depth of working collaboratively and the impact of the power imbalances between professional groups and professionals and their clients.

COLLABORATION IN PRACTICE

A further area which leads on from the language debate is in relation to who is involved in the collaboration. Is it just the professionals, in other words, those who perform the services, or does it include the recipients of their services, namely children and their families? The needs of those who use the services of health, education and social care are so varied that it is essential that they are active participants in the process so that professionals do not make assumptions about what they think their needs are (Leiba and Weinstein, 2003).

Indeed, working in collaboration with service users is recognized by policy makers and enshrined in legislation such as the Children Act 1989 and 2004; and UNCRC 1989. Working together should be for the benefit of both the service providers and those using the services. However, despite the area of service user participation growing in importance there is little research into the impact of service user involvement:

> The few studies summarized...indicate that genuine user involvement is patchy and very much dependent on individual champions of local circumstances. Progress is being made and most agencies have started policies and procedures for user involvement, although these vary in the comprehensiveness of their aims and the extent of implementation in practice.
>
> (Leiba and Weinstein, 2003: 67)

Further, Leiba and Weinstein (2003: 69) argue that there is a 'continuing concern about the quality of involvement, tokenism and lack of resources'. This situation must raise questions about how can we ensure a meaningful partnership between providers and 'consumers'. In relation to children and their families, if they are to be seen as active participants in the process with rights to receive services and input in their development, professionals need to recognize and actively value their involvement. Shaw (2000: 29) also raised the issue that researching into the value of service user involvement is 'still fairly novel'. However, if their views, opinions and experiences are to be valued then this position needs to be challenged. The question needs to be asked; how can we involve the service user in a meaningful way?

One way might be to assume that service users, client or patient are active participants. Loxley uses Cooperational Theory that assumes that people want to work together for their own benefit. She states:

> At an individual level the power of the client or patient to participate depends on the degree of choice available to him/her that is the person's power to reciprocate or withdraw. In a market-place such power is exercised as a consumer. In the public sector services, the pseudo-market creates purchasers who are agents for the users.

> (Loxley, 1997: 39)

Thus, how can the 'consumers' of care services have the same power they have when they are consumers of services in the market place? This is a challenging question and one which demands careful reflection. Valuing the service users' understanding and perception of their own needs has been the subject of much debate (Dominelli, 2002; Leiba and Weinstein, 2003).

For Leiba and Weinstein, 'service users are the most important participants in the collaborative process' (2003: 63). They view them as the 'experts' on their individual situations who have an opinion to give. They argue that 'one way of preventing carers from feeling marginalized and to make good use of the special understanding they have of the situation is to engage them fully' (2003: 66). However they highlight that some professionals can feel 'threatened' by this process and some service users 'uncomfortable'. They state that 'these anxieties must be recognized and opportunities provided to talk them through, if they are not to become barriers to change' (2003: 66). The concerns about using service users is also echoed by Thorpe (2004: 22) who discusses the fact that while service user involvement is seen as positive there are concerns 'that many policymakers and practitioners are only paying lip-service to the idea of user-driven services'. However, as Leiba and Weinstein (2003: 69) state: 'If we listen carefully to service users and carers...one of the things they tell us is that professionals should collaborate more effectively with each other. Absence of interprofessional collaboration causes breakdown in communication, delays in service delivery and general confusion and frustration for service users'.

While children and their families' involvement in the collaborative process is to be valued the power balance between them and the professionals also needs to be recognized especially when issues of care and control are at the forefront of working together. As Pinkerton (2001: 251) points out 'Child Protection work brings into particular sharp relief the difficulties there can be for partnership'. However, this power imbalance is not just evident in social work but in education and health as well. One way that the power imbalance is also highlighted is in relation to the name given to the people with whom professionals work. Indeed in this chapter the terms client and service user are interchanged, however, they can also be patients or even consumers of our services. An additional complication is the age of the person who is this 'consumer'. If it is a child at what age can they be involved in the partnership process for the dialogue to be meaningful? This leads on to the debate about whether it is the professional with all their knowledge, understanding and training that knows best or the child and or family being worked with. It is this area of knowledge that adds another area of complication to the collaborative process both for professionals and clients. Different members of the process may not value the role they have to play because they do not have the same qualifications or, indeed, social standing as other members of the partnership.

It is also important to recognize that collaboration needs effective communication. For Thompson (2003: 67) 'effective communication is not simply a matter of personal skills and individual efforts. Rather, it also depends on such important things as organizational systems, cultures and structures.' The specific nature of professional language adds a further complicating factor, different professions have their own language and set of abbreviations which can act as a barrier to communication; the same terminology can mean different things. For example, working in partnership in a school setting may refer to the agenda of working effectively with parents and, in a social care setting, working with other agencies and or clients (Braye, 2000). Therefore, if professionals struggle with communication how can service users hope to begin to engage in the process of collaboration.

There are, however, examples of positive strategies being developed to facilitate overcoming the language barriers. For example, the Sheffield Care Trust has developed a glossary of jargon for service users participating in council meetings (Thorpe, 2004). Another example is provided from the National Forum of People with Learning Difficulties, where a 'traffic light' card system is used. Everyone at the meeting has three cards: one used to stop people talking over them, one when they do not understand what is being discussed and another when they agree with what is being said (Leeson, 2004). While this method relates to people with learning difficulties it is a method that could be used with children and adults alike. Indeed, there are many occasions when this system would have benefited my understanding of a multiprofessional meeting.

If we are to move forward in relation to participation and actively involving children in the collaborative process professionals need to reflect on their language and think about different strategies that can be employed to break down the barriers (Thomas, 2000). Indeed, actively including children in this process of simplifying language can bring clarity to the fog in which adults sometimes find themselves. Mission statements are an example here as many organizations invest a considerable amount of time trying to find a way to summarize their existence. As a recent observer of a child participation council it was fascinating to see how one of the young participants reduced a two-paragraph mission statement to four words that encapsulated the meaning of the message succinctly. He went on to say that he could not understand why adults had to use so many words.

Thus, it is not surprising that the language of collaboration and how this collaboration translates into practice is challenging and complex. The growing literature in this area (Draper and Duffy, 2001; Harrison et al., 2004; Leeson and Griffiths, 2004; Loxley, 1997; Weinstein et al., 2003) raises issues around definition, interpretation and the interchangeable nature of the language used and who should be involved in the process. Despite the complexities in this area, it is clear that collaboration has been integral to different government's policies for several decades. As Leeson and Griffiths (2004) highlight, the work of Plowden (see Central Advisory Council for Education, 1967) drew attention to home–school links and Loxley (1997), provides a useful time line of documentation and legislation from 1971 onwards, where collaboration is included. Additionally, as stated at the beginning of this chapter, the latest government initiative for children and their families, *Every Child Matters: Change for Children* (Department for Education and Skills, 2004e) has services working effectively together as the challenge for the coming decade.

EFFECTIVE COLLABORATION

If the agenda of change for children is to move forward positively effective collaboration at all levels must be the goal strived for. As previously indicated while working together is not new, the challenge is to explore what are the ingredients that have worked well and use these as the basis for moving forward. There also needs to be acceptance that working in partnership with children and their families is constructive and that the gains from the process outweigh the difficulties that can occur. However, it is also important that this approach should not be used to mask the reasons why difficulties occur. Loxley (1997: 70–71) helpfully reminds us that:

> The appeal of teamwork, just as the appeal of collaboration, enables policy makers to avoid the crucial issues of irreconcilable structures and limited resources by laying on practitioners the responsibility of mitigating their effects, and practitioners can accept it without fully understanding or recognising that it contains unresolved contradictions. The myth serves to disguise the reality with an appealing ideology.

However, if we are to progress these issues need acknowledging so that participants in the process do not become resentful resulting in inaction by those involved. Rather, issues need to be aired openly and dealt with, thus freeing up the participants to focus on the specific task. This level of openness and honesty may not only help to improve the interpersonal relationships within the collaboration but enable a greater understanding of the positioning of those involved. It is in developing this understanding that degrees in early childhood can really make a difference as they can provide an arena in which students are able to develop their knowledge and understanding of the different professional roles in relation to children and their families. They also are afforded with the opportunity to develop key skills to take with them into the workplace, as the final section of this chapter will illustrate.

So how can we work towards effective collaboration? In order for the collaborative process to be successful there needs to be some common understanding between the participants. There also needs to be 'respect, reciprocity, realism and risk-taking' (Harrison et al., 2003: 26). Harrison et al. also usefully suggest the framework of 'SMART' (specific, measurable, achievable, relevant, timed) has a positive role to play. This allows purpose to be placed on the agenda by the participants at the start, they are able to consider how they will work together and how this can be measured. Harrison et al. (2003: 15) also liken the start of partnership to 'the first date', they provide a useful list of issues that participants need to consider (see Table 4.2).

Table 4.2 The first date

Before the meeting	At the meeting	After the meeting
Researching	Clarifying purpose	Finding the decision-makers
Sharing the idea	Recognizing mutual advantage	Gaining internal commitment
Planning an agenda	Identifying potential barriers	Drafting an agreement
Exploring the pros and cons	Anticipating how to get over the difficulties	Funding formula
Cost–benefit analysis	Drafting a proposal	Keeping an open mind

Source: Harrison et al., 2004: 15

Leeson and Griffiths (2004: 140) provide further insights into the ingredients for successful collaboration, including the importance of 'strengthening the emotional content of the relationship and interactions both inside and outside the working environments'. They also highlight management support, training and the importance of 'breaking down the power struggles among professionals'. I would suggest that the other important ingredient is the importance of a shared vision, a commitment to working together for the benefit of children and their families. In the early years this is in relation to a holistic approach to the child where professionals value and understand each other's positioning and relationship with the child and their families. Furthermore, the role of the 'consumers', whether a child or adult, of our services is valued and integrated into the collaboration process.

THE ROLE OF TRAINING IN EARLY YEARS

Along with government policy to alleviate child poverty and improve early years provision by working collaboratively, comes the need for a trained workforce (Abbott and Hevey, 2001; Department of Education and Skills, 2004e). Thus, over the next 10 years there will be workforce reforms and the growth in interest in the early years will mean that the early years courses that are becoming established in universities have a pivotal role to play.

The growth in early childhood studies degrees provides a real opportunity for students to engage in the widest debates about the early years from a health, social care and educational perspective. It affords them with the opportunity of seeing professionals from differing working and organizational cultures, with a different professional body of knowledge, different roles, different qualifications and salary scales, coming together and model good multiprofessional collaboration.

This development can only benefit the collaborative process. The first destination of students on early childhood courses is predominantly teaching. However, students from one early childhood studies degree clearly indicate that they have found the holistic nature of the study programme, where different perspectives are represented, invaluable in preparing them for their future careers (Murray and Lumsden, 2004). Indeed, many early years courses historically are based within a School of Education, however, by having a multidisciplinary approach to teaching means that staff from different backgrounds are coming together and working through the difficulties of their different roles and responsibilities for the child. It is also raising important questions about the balance of delivery of different perspectives and as students are engaging with health and social care they are becoming more vocal about the need for a balance between the three in the curriculum, regardless of their final career destinations. While this is an ongoing process the impact of the partnership has led to health and social care issues being integrated into other traditional education courses. This can help to the develop understanding of our respective positioning and roles in a child's journey into adulthood.

There has also been the development of the Early Years Sure Start Endorsed Foundation Degree, which awards senior practitioner status on successful candidates. This degree is attracting students from non-traditional routes and affords them the opportunity not only to develop their knowledge and understanding of the early year development and care of children but also to integrate this into the workplace. It is hoped that a high percentage of these students will develop the confidence to pursue their engagement with education further and convert their foundation degree into one with honours, thus opening the door to further opportunities such as the Postgraduate Certificate in Education; the graduate trainee route into teaching or an MA in Social Work and developing the workforce envisaged in *Every Child Matters: Change for Children* (Department of Education and Skills, 2004e).

SUMMARY

As this chapter has illustrated, working together is not a new concept and there are numerous examples of professionals already working together. However, the language of collaboration is complex both in relation to terminology and the players in the process. What is clear, is that for effective collaboration, those involved need to have a shared vision and a willingness to move beyond the complexities to enable a clear understanding of what each individual collaboration is aiming to achieve, how it is going to achieve it and how it will know when it has got there.

Every Child Matters means that the next 10 years will see collaboration and partnership more evident in practice. Professionals can no longer afford not to move outside the comfort zone of their own professional boundaries. Stepping outside and embracing other professionals, children and families is essential to develop a shared meaning for our engagement together and a workable process for successful collaboration.

One of the most important ways that this process will be facilitated is through improved training across professional boundaries. There needs to be a range of training initiatives that addresses the needs of a diverse workforce in education, health and social care. Degrees in early childhood provide one pathway, students develop knowledge and understanding about the different roles professionals play in a child's life. From this base of shared knowledge and understanding, students then have the opportunity to specialize in careers in education, health or social care.

The government needs to practically recognize the importance of valuing all those involved in the process both through ongoing, properly funded training, parity in pay scales and, indeed, pay incentives that value training undertaken. Every child does matter but in order to bring this vision to life training has to address the issues and provide practical ways in which children, their families and those working with them can develop effective collaborative practice.

QUESTIONS FOR REFLECTION AND DISCUSSION

1. What do you think are the issues that prevent professionals working together?
2. How do you think that training can promote positive collaborative practice?
3. Do you think the Children Act 2004 can really develop working together?
4. Can children and their carers ever be equal partners in the collaborative process?

Recommended reading

Calder, M. and Hackett, S. (eds) (2003) *Assessment in Child Care: Using and Developing Frameworks for Practice*. Lyme Regis: Russell House Publishing.

Department of Education and Skills (2004) *Every Child Matters: Change for Children*. London: HMSO. Available on: *http://www.everychildmatters.gov.uk*.

Harrison, R., Murphy, M., Taylor, A. and Thompson, N. (2003) *Partnership made Painless: A Joined Up Guide to Working Together*. Dorset: Russell House Publishing Ltd.

Loxley, A. (1997) *Collaboration in Health and Welfare: Working with Difference*. London: Jessica Kingsley Publishers Limited.

Sanders, B. (2004) 'Interagency and multidisciplinary working', in T. Maynard and N. Thomas (eds) *An Introduction to Early Childhood Studies*. London: Sage Publications.

Weinstein, J., Whittington, C. and Leiba, T. (eds) (2003) *Collaboration in Social Work Practice*. London: Jessica Kingsley Publishers.

Chapter 5

Modern childhood: contemporary theories and children's lives

Tim Waller

This chapter provides an overview of current international literature and research which underpins the study of early childhood. Much of the recent literature has been critical of the central role of 'child development' in theory concerning young children. In order to provide a contemporary account of the young child, the chapter identifies and critically discusses the following five key tenets of modern theory:

1. There are multiple and diverse childhoods
2. There are multiple perspectives of childhood
3. Children are involved in co-constructing their own childhood
4. Children's participation in family, community and culture makes a particular contribution to their life
5. We are still learning about childhood.

> Childhood may be defined as the life period during which a human being is regarded as a child, and the cultural, social and economic characteristics of that period.
>
> (Frones, 1994: 148)

This chapter provides an overview of current international literature and research which underpins the study of early childhood. Drawing from a range of recent sources (for example, BERA SIG, 2003; Riley, 2003; MacNaughton, 2003; Kehily, 2004; Maynard and Thomas, 2004; Penn, 2005) this chapter identifies five features of contemporary theories about children's 'development' and discusses their relevance to modern childhood. The explicit purpose of the chapter is therefore to explore alternative, contemporary views and not to repeat traditional texts (of which there are many) that consider children and childhood mainly from a psychological point of view.

Brown (1998), Moss (2001b) and MacNaughton (2003), for example, remind us of the importance of equity and the need to examine and question our own assumptions about children and childhood. It is common for adults to underestimate children. It is generally acknowledged that children are unique individuals, live in a social world, and that there is no such thing as 'normal' development (Donaldson, 1978; Dunn, 1988; Rose, 1989).

Moving towards a contemporary view of the child, the terms 'child' and 'child development' and, the whole concept of childhood have been questioned. Drawing on a range of perspectives, including the emerging sociology of childhood, the concept of childhood and the social history of children are examined and discussed and a holistic view is promoted. The chapter considers issues of equality and how they affect children and also focuses on children's participation in the family and community. Insights offered by recent research into early brain development are also evaluated.

THERE ARE MULTIPLE AND DIVERSE CHILDHOODS

A contemporary view acknowledges that childhood is not fixed and it is not universal, it is 'mobile and shifting' (Walkerdine, 2004). This means that children experience many different and varied childhoods. There are local variations and global forms, depending on class, 'race', gender, geography, time, etc. (see Penn, 2005 for a detailed discussion of alternative childhoods). Until recently, most of the published research and writing about children, childhood and child development has focused on individual development as a natural progress towards adulthood. This natural progress is conceived as the same for all children regardless of class, gender or 'race' (see MacNaughton, 2003: 73). Much of this considerable body of work, written from the perspective of psychology and developmental psychology, has promoted what Walkerdine (2004: 107) suggests is an 'essential childhood'. This is a traditional, western developmental view of the child, which is used to categorize all children throughout the world (Dahlberg, 1985; Walkerdine, 1993). Penn (2005), cites Rose (1989), who makes the point that a 'normal' child is a:

curious mix of statistical averages and historically specific value judgements. The most striking aspect of the 'normal' child is how abnormal he or she is, since there is no such person in reality and never has been. The advantage of defining normality is that it is a device that enables those in control or in charge to define, classify and treat those who do not seem to fit in.

(Penn: 2005: 7)

Over 95 per cent of this literature originates from the USA (Fawcett, 2000) and much of it has been written by men, or from a male perspective. Walkerdine (1993: 451) argues that so-called 'scientific' psychological 'truths' about child development 'have to be understood in terms of the historical circumstances in which the knowledge was generated'. For Walkerdine therefore, this knowledge has been generated in a patriarchal society and the story of child development is one that has been dominated by a male view. She argues strongly that relying on psychology to explain child development 'universalizes the masculine and European' (1993: 452).

Recently, due to the growing influence of a new sociology of childhood, cultural and anthropological studies, an alternative view which argues that childhood is an adult construction that changes over time and place has been put forward (see, for example, Gittins, 2004; Prout and James, 1990; James et al., 1998; Mayall, 2002). For MacNaughton (2003: 71) the development of the child is not a fact but a cultural construction. When we describe a child's development we are describing our cultural understandings and biases, not what exists in fact (Dahlberg et al., 1999).

As Penn (2005: 97) reminds us, 'the situation of most of the world's children is very different from those we study in North America and Europe'. The circumstances of the 80 per cent of the children who live in other parts of the world is significantly different in terms of wealth, health and culture (see Penn, 2005: 98–108).

1 in 6 children is severely hungry

1 in 7 no health care at all

1 in 5 has no safe water and 1 in 3 has no toilet or sanitation facilities at home

Over 640 million children live in dwellings with mud floors or extreme overcrowding

Over 120 million children are shut out of primary schools, the majority of them girls

180 million children work in the worst forms of child labour

1.2 million children are trafficked each year

2 million children, mostly girls, are exploited in the sex industry

Nearly half the 3.6 million people killed in conflict during the 1990s (45 per cent) were children

15 million children orphaned by AIDS, 80 per cent are African

(UNICEF: The State of the World's Children, 2004)

Further, the whole idea and usefulness of actually categorizing and studying something called 'child development' has recently been questioned (see Fawcett, 2000 for a more detailed critique). Clearly change and transformation happen throughout human life, but the argument is about how that change is understood and constituted. Dahlberg (1985) asserts that due to the central and dominant influence of developmental psychology our view of the child has been constrained to a scientific model of natural growth. Typically, this model of the child defines development in terms of a relatively narrow range of psychological aspects such as social, emotional and cognitive or intellectual and physical development. However, as Riley (2003:13) points out, these inter-related aspects are complex and developmentalism does not fully account for the complexity nor explain how they operate together in a holistic way. Zuckerman (1993: 239) also, argues that theories which suggest regular and predictable patterns of development oversimplify the reality of children's lives and actually hinder our understanding of childhood.

Dahlberg et al. (1999) also argue that development itself is a problematic term to apply to childhood because it produces oppressive practices. Walkerdine (1993) and Silin (1995) argue that our perspectives on the child have contributed to their oppression and exploitation in different ways because we are in a process of judging their differences to us as inadequacies or weaknesses rather than alternative ways of knowing (Silin, 1995: 49). MacNaughton (2003: 75) discusses this point and cites Cannella (1997: 64) who asserts that, 'child development is an imperialist notion that justifies categorising children and diverse cultures as backward and needing help from those who are more advanced'.

However, while there is an argument for the recognition of the social construction of childhood and the emerging sociology of childhood, as articulated above and in the section below, this is only one of multiple perspectives of childhood. Walkerdine (2004), for example, rightly questions the place of modern accounts of childhood that replace psychological understandings of individual development with sociological interpretations that focus on 'how child subjects are produced' (2004: 96). She argues that this 'dualism' replaces internal views of the child with external and that child development has a place. Considering childhood as a simple progression through defined stages is, however, too simplistic. There are multiple and diverse childhoods and in order to study childhood one has to consider a range of perspectives.

THERE ARE MULTIPLE PERSPECTIVES OF CHILDHOOD

A number of alternative and multiple perspectives can be drawn on to explain contemporary childhood (Walkerdine, 2004). These perspectives are culturally influenced and change over time. As Kehily (2004: 1) points out, different disciplines have for a long time developed different ways of approaching the study of children. Recently, however, a growing body of international work from the perspective of sociology (James and Prout, 1997; Mayall, 2002), early childhood education (MacNaughton, 2003), critical theory and feminism (Walkerdine, 1993) and cultural studies (Cole, 1996) has been critical of the place of developmental psychology in producing explanations of children as potential subjects, whose presence is only understood in terms of their place on a path towards becoming an adult (Walkerdine, 2004: 96). A current understanding of children's development is, therefore, that it can be approached from a variety of perspectives and that these perspectives are culturally influenced and change over time.

James and Prout (1997: 8) identified the following key features of the 'new sociology of childhood':

- childhood is understood as a social construction
- childhood is a variable of social analysis
- children's relationships and cultures are worthy of study in their own right
- children are active social agents
- studying childhood involves engagement with the process of reconstructing childhood in society.

They suggest that 'the immaturity of children is a biological fact of life but the ways in which this immaturity is understood and made meaningful is a fact of culture'. For Cunningham (1995: 3), 'childhood cannot be studied in isolation from society as a whole'. In contemporary culture childhood has become a formal category with a social status, and seen as an important stage in development. This status has been given boundaries by our society's institutions; families, clinics, early years settings and schools, etc. Jenks (1982) and Hoyles and Evans (1989) infer that this analysis places 'childhood' within a social construct, rather than a natural phenomenon.

The idea of childhood as a separate state to adulthood is a modern one. Aries (1962: 152) argues that very little distinction between children and adults was made until sometime around the fifteenth century: 'in mediaeval society childhood did not exist'. From the fifteenth century onwards children began to appear as children, reflecting their gradual removal from everyday adult society. Then, following the advent of compulsory schooling in the late nineteenth century (in Europe), the specific category of 'childhood' was produced, constructed (Aries, 1962) and institutionalized (Walkerdine, 1993).

Alternatively, Pollock (1983) suggests that it is mistaken to believe that because a past society did not possess the contemporary western view of childhood, that society had no such concept. Even if children were regarded differently in the past this does not mean that they were not regarded as children. However, he does acknowledge that the particular form of modern childhood is historically specific. Historical studies of childhood suggest that, in the UK, childhood was re-conceptualized between the end of the nineteenth century and the start of World War I Gittins, 1998). These studies demonstrate a significant shift in the economic and sentimental value of children. Over a fairly short period working-class children changed from one of supplementing the family income to that of a relatively inactive member of the household in economic terms to be protected from the adult world of hardship (Cunningham, 1995). Zelitzer (1985) argues that children's contributions to the family in western contexts is economically worthless but emotionally 'priceless'. Children's value lies in their ability to give meaning and fulfilment to their parents lives.

Alwin (1990) points out that the distinct category of childhood arose out of attitudinal shifts that placed children in the centre of the family and encouraged an affectionate bond between parents and their children. Thus, for Alwin, childhood is defined by four criteria: protection, segregation, dependence and delayed responsibility. Further, Gittins (2004) argues that the development of childhood as a concept was class-specific, reflecting the values and practices of a rising European middle-class that increasingly differentiated adults and children, girls and boys.

Views of childhood, therefore, *have changed* and *are changing*. The main factors impacting childhood are; economic, demographic, cultural and political. Since 1945, as a result of economic conditions in the West and the increase of compulsory schooling to the age of sixteen, a 'teenage' culture involving clothes, music, media and films has been constructed. Teenagers are defined by their potential spending power and targeted by advertising in the same way as adults. More recently, a further group of 'tweenagers' or 'tweenies' have been distinguished (*The Guardian*, 2001). These are defined as seven to twelve-year-olds who already show teenage tendencies. For example, seven to twelve-year-old girls who currently shop for 'designer' clothes wear make up and own mobile phones.

There is also a growing recognition of the impact of digital technology on children's lives (see, for example Buckingham, 2000; Facer et al., 2002; Labbo et al., 2000; Luke, 1999; Yelland, 1999). They argue that it is important to consider how the development of the personal computer, computer games and access to digital communications technology such as email and the internet has affected children's experiences and relationships between children and adults. While Postman (1983) predicted that computer use would lead to greater divisions between children and adults, this has not appeared to be the case. Many children have become experts in using technology and are able to access and use information in different ways as a result (see Heppell, 2000; Luke, 1999). Yelland (1999), also, argues that we need to take account of the child's perspective of electronic media.

CHILDREN ARE INVOLVED IN CO-CONSTRUCTING THEIR OWN CHILDHOOD

While a child is clearly biologically determined as a young person, a 'child' is also socially determined in time, place, economics and culture. There is debate about the role of adults in this social construction of childhood and the agency of children in their own lives. Mayall (1996: 1), for example, has argued that, 'children's lives are lived through childhoods constructed for them by adults' understanding of childhood and what children are and should be'. Currently there is an acknowledgement of the significance of the dimension of power in relations between children and adults, and the impact of this relationship on our concept of, study and understanding of children and childhood (Riley, 2003). As Connell (1987) points out, power sometimes involves the direct use of force but it is always also accompanied by the development of ideas (ideologies) which justify the actions of the powerful. Canella (2001) argues that adult/child categories create an ageism that privileges adult's meanings over those of children.

Alderson (2005: 129) draws on gender studies to identify and emphasize the significance of these adult definitions and ideas in the lives of all children. The columns in Table 5.1 relate to what women and men were assumed to be like and Column 1 can also be applied to how children are perceived and presented in traditional child development literature and adult constructs of the child.

Table 5.1 'Half people'

Column 1 – women	Column 2 – men
Ignorant	Knowing
Inexperienced	Experienced
Volatile	Stable
Foolish	Wise
Dependent	Protective
Unreliable	Reliable
Weak	Stong
Immature	Mature
Irrational	Rational
Incompetent	Competent

Source: Alderson, 2005: 129

Alderson (2005: 131) argues that:

- children often seem weak and ignorant because they are kept in helpless dependence
- children who try to move to Column 2 may be punished
- they are not allowed to gain knowledge and experience
- it suits adults to keep Column 2 for themselves.

While there are many recent examples of literature that promotes positive views of competent children, Alderson argues that there is a problem, especially with older approaches, that emphasize negative stereotypes of children (based on Column 1) because of their age.

A modern view of the child acknowledges agency, that is, children's capacity to understand and act upon their world. It acknowledges that children demonstrate extraordinary competence from birth. It is informed by Malaguzzi's (1993: 10) concept of the 'rich child'. The child who is 'rich in potential, strong, powerful and competent'. This perspective sees the child as actively participating in her own childhood (Riley, 2003: 15). This view also asserts that while adults have power, children have power to resist that power. Hendrick (1997: 59) makes a significant point about the agency of the child. He argues that changes in the conception of childhood did not just happen, they were contested and not least important among the contestants were the children themselves.

Mayall (2002: 21) suggests that children are best regarded as a minority social group and she locates children's agency within the restriction of this minority status. Mayall (1994, 2002) does, however, acknowledge the significant role that children play in providing support and making and maintaining relationships in families. She recognizes children 'as agents, with specific views on the institutions and adults they interact with' (1996: 2). A number of recent writers (for example Corsaro, 1997; Qvortrup et al., 1994) go further and have argued that children are active agents who construct their own cultures. Children have their own activities, their own time and their own space (Qvortrup et al., 1994: 4). For example, Pollard's (2000) study on the agency of children at primary school in England showed how children learn to survive and cope with school through their own culture and the support of their peer group. 'Breaktime' is seen as a particularly significant site, providing the time and location for children's culture (see Blatchford, 1998).

Children's views of their own childhood are therefore particularly significant. As Lloyd-Smith and Tarr (2000: 66) point out, the Children Act (1989) in the UK established the right of the child to be listened to. An important aspect is children's own views of their daily experience. Qvortrup et al. (1994: 2) argue that 'children are often denied the right to speak for themselves either because they are held incompetent in making judgements or because they are thought of as unreliable witnesses about their own lives'. Thomas (2001:104) suggests that listening to children is important because:

● they have the right to be heard
● it can enhance their welfare
● it leads to better decisions.

Thomas argues that if there is presumption of competence, rather than incompetence, children often turn out to be more capable and sophisticated than they are given credit for. He suggests that the advantages of working with a presumption of competence and respect for children and what they wish to communicate are apparent in both childcare work and social research (2001: 110). However, Hill (1999) cited in Stainton-Rogers (2004: 140), makes the point that attempts to discover the views of parents as service users is only a recent trend and, in social care, it is even more unusual for children to be consulted.

Stainton-Rogers (2004) discusses the different perspectives of parents and children. It is clear from interviews with children (Pollard, 2000; Mayall, 2002, etc.) that parents' priorities are quite different to those of children. Stainton-Rogers (2004: 140) gives the example of parents' views of schools being concerned with performance and appearance ('league tables' and the physical environment), whereas children are concerned about social interaction and self-esteem (being treated with respect and not bullied). Parents expressed concern about their children facing external threats from traffic, being abducted by strangers and violence on the street – but children are most concerned about tension and conflict with peers. Research and literature by Carr (2001, *Children's Learning Stories*) and Clark and Moss (2001, *The Mosaic Approach*) for example, demonstrates the value and potency of listening to children.

MacNaughton (2004: 46) suggests that 'children make their own meanings, but not under conditions of their own choosing'. MacNaughton (2004: 47) identifies four 'conditions of power' that impact on children:

1 The power of pre-existing cultural imagery and cultural meanings.
2 The power of expectations.
3 The power of positions.
4 The power of the marketplace.

MacNaughton argues that children enter a pre-existing world in which each of these conditions of power is already accomplished. As an example she discusses the children's entertainment and toy industry to show how global capital produces the material culture through which children construct their meanings. However, as Riley (2003: 14) points out, children are powerful consumers in the multi-million dollar industry of childhood that is focused around clothes, toys, books and electronic and digital media (see Luke, 1999; Buckingham, 2004).

Thus, while there is some debate in contemporary literature about the effect of adult power on childhood, children are seen as actively involved in the co-construction of their own lives. A modern explanation of childhood therefore seeks to understand the definitions and meaning children give to their own lives and recognizes children's competence and capacity to understand and act upon their world.

CHILDREN'S PARTICIPATION IN FAMILY, COMMUNITY AND CULTURE MAKES A PARTICULAR CONTRIBUTION TO THEIR OWN LIFE

Much of the recent literature in the field of early childhood argues that there is a need to consider the wider political, social and cultural context of childhood. Bronfenbrenner (1977) acknowledged a range of contextual factors that impact directly and indirectly on the development of a child in his concept of ecological systems (see Berk, 2000 for a more detailed discussion). Ecological systems theory represents the child's development as multilayered and the benefit of this model is that it places the child and the child's experience at the heart of the process of development. While it is a useful framework, it can be used to imply that context is something that impacts *on* the child, rather than *with* and *through* the child's participation. It does not fully articulate agency and co-construction.

The recent influential work of proponents of the socio-cultural or 'situative perspective' such as Rogoff (1998, 2003), will now be briefly considered (the social construction of learning is discussed in further detail in Chapter 7). The socio-cultural perspective has adapted and enhanced the ideas of Vygotsky (1978, 1986) and provided valuable new insights into the collaborative nature of learning and the social construction of knowledge. It has been particularly influential in the field of early childhood. This perspective takes into account not just the child but the social, historical, institutional and cultural factors in which the child is participates in and co-constructs. It recognizes that human activity is heavily influenced by *context*, which includes artefacts, and other people. The socio-cultural approach also emphasizes the shared construction and distribution of knowledge leading to the development of shared understanding and common knowledge (Greeno, 1997; Lave, 1988; Edwards and Mercer, 1987; Rogoff, 1990; Pea, 1993). As a result, the child is not seen as an individual learner but as a participant in a range of meaningful and instructional social practices. Learning and development are inseparable from the concerns of families and interpersonal and community processes. This is a dynamic and evolving cultural context, in which it is meaningless to study the child apart from other people. Participation, as contrasted with acquisition, is therefore a key concept here.

WE ARE STILL LEARNING ABOUT CHILDREN AND CHILDHOOD

If children are active participants in dynamic and evolving cultural contexts, as argued above, it follows that we will always be learning about children and childhood. In addition, changes in technology and new methods of investigation and research can also generate new areas of knowledge and understanding. One aspect of young children's progress that has received considerable attention over the last 10 years is early brain development (BERA SIG 2003: 18). Following recent advances in computer technology leading to the development of brain imaging techniques, such as Functional Magnetic Resonance Imaging (fMRI) and Positron Emission Tomography (PET) scans, neuroscientists have been able to measure activity in the brain and map the growth of the brain (Blakemore, 2000). However, there has been a debate surrounding the implications of this neuroscientific research for education and care in the early years (BERA SIG 2003: 18).

What the research has usefully shown is that there is a very rapid increase in the development of the brain for young children, especially those under three years of age Riley (2003: 3). The brain appears as early as the third week after conception (27 days) and develops rapidly, so that by end of the seventh month of pregnancy the baby's brain has all the neurons of the adult brain and many to spare (Catherwood, 1999). Crucial are the synapses – the connections between cells (neurons) where information is exchanged. Most development of synapses occurs after birth, however, at birth the neonate has approximately half the number of synapses of the adult brain. Very rapid growth then occurs from 2–4 months, so that by 6 months baby has more synapses than an adult. Stimulation from the environment causes 'learning' either by stabilizing existing networks in the brain or by forging new ones. The ability of the brain to develop connections (or synapses) is known as plasticity. Recent brain research (Blakemore, 2000) has revealed that, after the age of three, plasticity continues at a slower rate until the age of ten.

Debate has focused on the possibility of 'critical periods' for learning, when plasticity is greatest. The argument is that if children do not have certain experiences during these critical periods, they will forever miss the opportunity to benefit from the experience. For this reason some writers (such as, Brierley, 1994; Sylwester, 1995) advocate 'hot-housing'. For example, starting to teach music to children under three, because the brain is so receptive to learning early on (see Blakemore, 2000). Bruer (1997), however, argues that making links between cognitive neuroscience and education is 'a bridge too far' and Blakemore and Frith (2000: 2) point out that brain research does not necessarily suggest the need to rush to start teaching earlier – indeed late starts may be considered to be in tune with the research.

A major assertion as a result of new information on early brain activity and growth was the acknowledgement of the extent to which the quality of early experience influences a child's later development. Because the vast majority of synapses are formed during the first three years of life and reduce after the age of 10, these first three years are seen as critical. However, it is now argued that while there are optimal 'windows of opportunity' for the development of synapses in the first three years, the brain is extremely flexible. An individual's capacities are therefore not fixed at birth, or in the first three years of life (Bransford et al., 2000).

Bransford et al. (2000) review the work of 16 leading researchers in cognitive science in the USA. Key conclusions from this evidence suggest, according to BERA SIG (2003: 18), that learning changes the structure of the brain; learning organizes and reorganizes the brain and different parts of the brain may be ready to learn at different times. Thus, although there are prime times for certain types of learning, the brain also has a remarkable capacity to change.

BERA SIG (2003: 19) also usefully summarizes evidence from brain research that matches with psychological research as follows:

1 Experience – everything that goes on around the young child changes the brain.
2 Everything the baby sees, hears, touches and smells influences the developing network of connections among the brain cells.
3 Other people play a critical role.
4 Babies and young children have powerful learning capacities.
5 They actually participate in building their own brain.
6 Radically deprived environments may influence development.

SUMMARY

This chapter has identified and discussed five key tenets of contemporary childhood. The tenets have articulated a complex model of childhood which is fundamentally different from a narrow 'developmental' approach. This model acknowledges that there are multiple and diverse childhoods. There are local variations and global forms, depending on class, 'race', gender, geography and time. This model also acknowledges that while there are multiple perspectives of childhood, it would be wrong to ignore or disregard developmental insights. Views of childhood have changed and are changing. Students of early childhood need to understand how and why child development theory is a product of certain historical, cultural and economic conditions. Some theoretical perspectives are particularly suited to explaining certain aspects of growth and change over time but the complex and interlinked nature of children's 'development' needs to be recognized. Developmental psychology should be studied alongside sociological, historical and anthropological accounts of childhood.

However, a critical difference between contemporary and traditional views of childhood is that the former recognizes the differing contexts of children's lives, children's agency and the significance of children's involvement in co-constructing their own childhood through participation in family, community and culture.

After 150 years of recognized child study we are still learning about children and childhood, the power of adults and the ability of children to determine their own future. Greater recognition of children's perspectives, the impact of new technology on children's lives and research methods will lead to further insights that will strengthen understanding and articulate new theories of early childhood.

QUESTIONS FOR REFLECTION AND DISCUSSION

1. How do children shape their own development?
2. How does change occur?
3. How do children become so different from each other?
4. How can you find out?
5. How should we deal with theories that do not recognize multiple and diverse childhoods and the power relationships between children and adults?

Recommended reading

Dahlberg, G., Moss, P. and Pence, A. (1999) *Beyond Quality in Early Childhood Education and Care: Postmodern Perspectives.* London and New York: RoutledgeFalmer.

James, A. and Prout, A. (eds) (1997) *Constructing and Reconstructing Childhood: Contemporary Issues in the Sociological Study of Childhood.* London: RoutledgeFalmer.

MacNaughton, G. (2003) *Shaping Early Childhood.* Maidenhead: Open University Press.

Penn, H. (2005) *Understanding Early Childhood.* Maidenhead: Open University Press.

Rogoff, B. (1990) *Apprenticeship in Thinking: Cognitive Development in Social Context.* New York: Plenum Press.

Chapter 6

Child health

Sharon Smith and Tania Morris

This chapter discusses the state of child health in the UK. It considers a holistic view of health and consequently explores physical, emotional and mental well-being in children. Relevant social policy and socio-economic influences are considered including the recent National Service Framework (2004) for Children. Case studies and practice examples are used throughout to illustrate implementation of health programmes.

Evidence suggests that children are generally healthier than ever before although this improving picture is marred by stark and persistent inequalities in health between children from advantaged families and those who are poor; across different ethnic groups and across different parts of the country. Healthy mothers produce healthy babies who become healthy children and adults; much preventable adult ill health and disease has its roots during gestation, infancy and childhood.

Children's health has been a major focus of recent government policy and is a priority not only in relation to health services, but also with respect to social services and education (Hill and Morton, 2003). Much interest in child health is due to the desire to influence later adult health. Many serious and life-threatening illnesses in adulthood are now seen as having their roots in life style choices with respect to diet, exercise, alcohol and substance use, which originate in childhood (Rigby, 2002). Changing patterns of eating, playing, working, travel and leisure activities have together led to an unhealthy lifestyle for some children that continues into adolescence and adulthood (DoH, 2004).

Children and young people are frequent users of all types of health care compared with adults. In a typical year, a pre-school child will see their general practitioner about six times, while a child of school age will go two or three times. Up to half of all infants aged less than 12 months and one-quarter of older children will attend an A & E Department. However, 80 per cent of all episodes of illness in children are managed by parents without reference to the professional health care system. This is important to note in relation to health promotion and support for parents.

The recently published National Service Framework for Children, Young People and Maternity Services (DoH, 2004) is a 10-year pro-gramme intended to stimulate long-term and sustained improvement in children's health. It is part of the government's overall plan for tackling child poverty which will be discussed further in this chapter. It is intended to lead to a cultural shift, resulting in services which are designed and delivered around the needs of children and families using those services, not around the needs of organizations. There are three key objectives:

1 To put children and their families at the centre of care.
2 To develop effective partnership working.
3 To deliver needs-led services.

The NSF will have a key role in helping to achieve the outcomes identi-fied by *Every Child Matters* (DES, 2004e):

● be healthy
● stay safe
● enjoy and achieve
● make a positive contribution
● achieve economic well-being.

Too often services neglect to see the child as the 'whole' person with basic developmental, physical mental and social needs that are very dif-ferent from those of an adult. Seeing the whole child also means recognizing that health protection and promotion and disease preven-tion are integral to their care in any setting. The child exists in a context

– family, friends, and school and, therefore, it is essential to remember that if care is optimal the child will avoid missing school to avoid problems with social functioning, friendships, etc.

This chapter will examine key aspects of child health promotion and disease prevention. The role of primary health care practitioners and educationalists will be discussed in the belief that education and health go hand in hand both impacting on children's current and future well-being. The support of families, especially those in special circumstances, and effective parenting interventions will be explored. There is increasing evidence to suggest that there is a strong association between aspects of family relationships, parenting behaviour and child behaviour problems (Johnston et al., 2004). It is widely recognized that early intervention is more effective and that health visitors and school nurses are in a strategically important position to deliver behaviour treatment, often more acceptable to families than a mental health service.

ROLE OF PRIMARY HEALTH CARE PRACTITIONERS

As key public health and primary care practitioners, health visitors and school nurses have an important role to play in improving child health and tackling inequalities. The significance of their contribution was highlighted in *Saving Lives: Our Healthier Nation* (1998) and *Making a Difference* (1999) which set out a child-centred public health role for working with children, families and schools.

Health need can be responded to in a variety of ways including individual and family health programmes, for example, breast feeding support or counselling for post-natal depression. The provision of and promotion of access to information services such as Sure Start programmes, Parentline and health-related websites can have a positive impact on family health need. Community development initiatives can meet local health needs and promote community participation, e.g. smoking cessations, healthy schools projects and safety schemes.

CASE STUDY

A teacher identified that a pupil with eczema was reluctant to attend swimming lessons at school because he complained that he felt uncomfortable afterwards. The school nurse identified in his child health plan how swimming was irritating the condition and making it difficult for him to concentrate at school. The school nurse, parent and teacher discussed how they could offer more time and support to enable him to enable him to be able to dry his skin carefully and reapply protective lotions. They agreed to assess the effect of the agreed plan over the following two weeks.

When discussing family issues the parent revealed that an older sibling was missing appointments at the local hospital's enuresis clinic. From a number of child health plans the school nurse knew that this was a problem as the clinic was difficult to reach and young people did not want to miss school in order to go for treatment. Further investigation suggested venues in their local community would be accessible. As a result a nurse-led service has been developed locally offering advice, periodic review and reordering of clinical supplies more conveniently (DoH, 2001a).

ROLE OF HEALTH VISITORS

Health visitors have a strong tradition of working with individuals, families and communities to promote health. Cowley and Houston (2003) recognize the different elements:

- public health programmes at community level
- community development
- group work
- health prevention and promotion with families and individuals.

They maintain a caseload of all families in a local area who have children under the age of five years delivering their service through a combination of individualized home visiting, clinic contacts and community-based activities.

WORKING WITH FAMILIES

The family in all its diverse forms is the basic unit of society and the place where the majority of health care and preventative work takes place. Health visitors have always played a vital role in promoting family health and supporting parents. *The Acheson Report* (1998) and the *NHS Plan* (2000) recognize the importance of working with families with young children to improve the life time chances of those in the poorest sections of the population. *Supporting Families* (1998) also highlighted the importance of health visitors' support role in improving child and family health and well-being.

The Family Health Plan (DoH, 2001b) supports this work and provides a tool to assess family health needs and plan services to meet these needs. A family health plan is a core tool for enabling a family to think about their health and parenting needs. Too often services neglect to see the child as the 'whole person' with basic developmental, physical, mental and social needs that are very different from those of an adult. Seeing the whole child also means recognizing that health protection and promotion and disease prevention are integral to their care in any setting.

The plan should identify:

● the family's health needs
● how they wish to address them
● an action plan (including multiprofessional support).

Health visitors aim to balance assessment of health need from both the community and individual health perspective working with other agencies and sectors to plan services and promote well-being. The content of this plan will form the framework for key health promotion areas to be explored.

ROLE OF SCHOOL NURSES

School nurses have an important role to play in improving health and tackling inequalities. The significance of their contribution was highlighted in *Saving Lives: Our Healthier Nation* (1998) and *Making a Difference* (1999) which set out a child-centred public health role for school nurses working with children, young people, families and school.

School nurses can provide a unique insight into the health needs of the school community and can provide a range of health improvement activities including:

- immunization and vaccination programmes
- support and advice to teachers and other school staff on a range of child health issues
- support and counselling in positive mental health
- personal health and social education programmes and citizenship training
- advice on relationships and sex education
- working with parents and other professionals to meet the range of health and social needs.

CASE STUDY

A healthy school survey showed that children wanted more activities, school nurses reported that children were inactive, the rates of coronary heart disease locally were high and the education development plan identified behaviour management as an issue to be tackled. School nurses became involved with physical education advisers in training non-teaching staff to provide traditional and active games at break times. Children reported that they enjoyed the physical activities, and staff observed that there was a notable improvement in concentration during lessons. Further evaluations demonstrated reduced behaviour management incidents at break time (DoH, 2001a).

The development of National Service Frameworks (NSF) Primary Care Trusts and new models of service delivery such as the National Health School Standard (NHSS) give school nurses opportunities to focus on the most important issues affecting children and young people's health and to work with population groups in greatest need. *The National Health Schools Standards* (1999) are part of the government's strategy to raise the educational achievement and address inequalities.

The Primary Schools/Primary Care Health Links Project aims specifically to promote the involvement of primary health care professionals in supporting children's learning and development in the context of the local healthy schools programme.

What is a healthy school?

A healthy school understands the importance of investing in health to assist in the process of raising levels of pupil achievement and improving standards. It promotes physical and emotional health by providing accessible and relevant information and equipping pupils with the skills and attitudes to make informed decisions about their health. It also recognizes the need to provide both a physical and social environment that is conducive to learning

(NHSS, 2001)

A systematic review of healthy schools (Lister-Sharp et al., 1999) concluded that school-based health promotion initiatives can have a positive impact on children's health and development.

CHILD HEALTH PROMOTION

A variety of factors affect health in children, not only biological and lifestyle problems of the parents, including unemployment, low income and poor housing. Health promotion can be defined as 'any planned and informed intervention which is designed to improve physical or mental health or to prevent disease' (Hall and Elliman, 2004).

A number of child health promotion activities will be explored including immunization, nutrition, physical activity and mental health.

Immunization

Protecting children against infectious disease has always been a cornerstone of public health work (Diggle, 2004). Health professionals play an essential role in ensuring that children are protected by giving parents evidence-based advice, within a flexible, convenient and high quality immunization service. This commitment to immunization by health professionals is vital amid some medical advertising campaigns which display confusion and often ill-informed scare stories. This has resulted in a lower uptake of vaccines in recent years (Macdonald, 2004). Other examples of factors associated with low uptake are family size (Taylor, 1993), lone parenting (Sharland, 1997) and in rural areas, access to transport (Wilson, 2000).

The re-establishment of parental confidence in the MMR vaccine will require considerable time and effort. Many professionals believe there needs to be more extensive publicity about the studies that do provide measurable evidence of there being no association between autism and MMR and enable both practitioners and parents to make a true evaluation of the risk. Table 6.1 shows the schedule for childhood vaccinations.

Table 6.1   Schedule of childhood vaccinations

Age	Vaccine
2 months	Diphtheria/Tetanus/Acellular Pertussis/Inactivated Polio/Hib (Haemophilus influenzae type B) (combined as one injection) Meningococcal C (given as a separate injection)
3 months	Diphtheria/Tetanus/Acellular Pertussis/Inactivated Polio/Hib (combined as one injection) Meningococcal C (given as a separate injection)
4 months	Diphtheria/Tetanus/Acellular Pertussis/Inactivated Polio/Hib (combined as one injection) Meningococcal C (given as a separate injection)
Around 13 months	Measles/Mumps/Rubella (combined as one injection)
Pre-school booster (between 3 years 4 months and 5 years)	Booster of Diphtheria/Tetanus/Acellar Pertussis/Inactivated Polio (combined as one injection) 2nd dose of Measles/Mumps/Rubella

Source: DoH, 2004

Nutrition

There is increasing concern regarding the relationship between the current state of childhood nutrition and adverse health outcomes in adult life (Hall and Elliman, 2004). What we eat in childhood affects our health, e.g. adults with coronary heart disease, diabetes, cancer and bowel disorders being attributed to the effects of poor diet in the early years. Recent research has indicated higher levels of obesity in children resulting from diets high in fat and sugar, combined with reduced activity levels (Gregory, 2000). Many of these inappropriate dietary patterns are also known to adversely affect iron status (iron deficiency anaemia) and dental health. Dental caries results frequently from excessive consumption of sweets, biscuits and sugared drinks between meals, especially drinks given in a bottle. Health visitors have an important role in promoting breastfeeding and in ensuring children progress through weaning to a balanced, varied diet (Parry and Jowett, 2001).

School nurses can improve nutrition among school age children. Nutrition is a key theme within the National Healthy School Standard, for example, the National Fruit School Scheme enabling access to fruit at school for all children. Easier access to drinking water in schools is promoted as part of the 'water is cool in school' campaign.

Although the recommended intake of fruit and vegetables is at least five portions a day, the current UK average daily consumption for children is two portions (MAFF, 1997). White's (2003) study suggests the main barriers to intake of fruit and vegetable are lack of availability, low income, transport problems, and lack of preparation, cooking knowledge and skills. Hall and Elliman (2004) support the need to encourage food related initiatives in schools – for example, breakfast clubs, food growing schemes that involve children in their planning.

CASE STUDY

A healthy school survey identified food issues as a health improvement priority. The school profile showed a high incidence of tooth decay from the early years. Packed lunches are brought by 33 per cent of the children. Monitoring the lunch times over a week, the school nurse and lunch time organizer observed that 70 per cent of the drinks were of a high sugar content. The sale of school milk had declined over recent years – children complained it was not cold. The healthy school team set a target to reduce high sugar drinks in packed lunches by 50 per cent within three terms.

The school nurse offered to take the lead, working in collaboration with parents, children and outside agencies to achieve this target (DoH, 2001a).

Promoting physical activity

There appears to be declining levels of activity among children particularly girls. The National Health School Standards (NHSS) recommends two hours' physical activity a week per pupil whatever their age or ability, within or outside the national curriculum. It is suggested (Hall and

Elliman, 2004) that measures could be implemented to enhance exercise levels and reduce the risk of obesity. These include:

- making school playgrounds safer and more enjoyable so that children can be more active
- increasing access to exercise (e.g. investment in road safety schemes to promote walking and cycling, free or low-cost sports facilities)
- promoting reduced traffic speeds and introduce traffic calming or diversion so that children can play outside
- reducing television viewing
- increasing accessibility and affordability of facilities for children and young people outside the home (swimming pools, skating rinks, and clubs).

Regular physical activity has important health benefit for children including:

- reducing the risk of heart disease and osteoporosis in adult life
- reducing hypertension
- playing a significant part in reducing obesity
- enhancing academic performance
- providing important social opportunities and attitudes towards physical activity (DoH, 2001a).

Mental illness in children

All children from time to time feel sad, anxious, angry, or upset – it is part and parcel of growing up. Some children will be able to talk about the way they feel, others may express their feelings through moody behaviour or by becoming difficult to control. However sometimes abnormalities of emotions, behaviour or social relationships may lead to potentially serious difficulties, risking the child's optimal physical, psychosocial development, which can result in the child's family unit being disturbed and in some cases impact upon their local community (DOH, 2004). Research has shown that 10 per cent of 5 to 10-year-old children may be suffering from some degree of mental or emotional problem (Meltzer et al., 2000), with many of those children needing professional help, and a proportion of these children experiencing continuing problems into adulthood (Caspi et al., 1996).

Factors that may indicate that a child is susceptible to mental health problems are varied; sometimes a direct cause can be linked to the child's mental health problems. In other cases the child's problems may be multifactorial. Predisposing factors may be evident such as brain injury, prior, during or after birth, or previous physical illness, or a genetic or biological vulnerability. Precipitating factors may also increase the child's susceptibility to mental health problems, these factors may include; parental conflict, family breakdown; physical, sexual or emotional abuse; bereavement/loss of family or friend, rejecting or hostile relationships or discrimination (Public Health Institute of Scotland, 2003). Research suggests that perpetuating factors may also increase the child's vulnerability of experiencing emotional difficulties, for example, economic disadvantage (Maughan et al., 1999); homelessness (Craig and Hodson, 1998); parental psychiatric illness (Carr, 2000); domestic violence (Abrahams, 1994; Webb, 2001) and alcoholism (Velleman and Templeton, 2003). However, of note is that in some cases less obviously traumatic events, such as moving house, the arrival of a new baby or being left for a long time with someone a child does not know, can cause long-term distress.

Arguably, all children and young people have to deal with a range of factors, which put their mental health at risk, for example, bereavement, divorce and separation. However, some suggest resilience of some children may be due to protective factors in their environment, e.g. a loving parent, a special teacher, a strong community (Public Health Institute of Scotland, 2003). The resilience of some children without these protective factors continues to baffle the experts.

Mental illness in children exhibits itself in varied ways. For example, some of the common manifestations of psychological problems are appetite, sleep and elimination problems. These include, excessive 'clinginess', crying, loss of confidence and withdrawal and inability to concentrate. Psychosomatic problems may be manifested such as headaches or stomach pains. Behavioural problems may occur, for example, demanding or destructive behaviour, clumsiness, carelessness or irritability, temper tantrums or hyperactivity, with the child being very hard to control. Learning difficulties may be detectable. All these signs are indications of possible psychological distress. Many children experiencing this type of distress find it hard to talk and will often show their feelings through behaviour. For example, a school-age child may lose interest in work and play and refuse to go to school, playing truant may be a sign that the child is unhappy.

Notably babies do not exhibit the classic symptoms of mental illness and disorder, however, they may exhibit poor sleep patterns, difficulties with feeding, restlessness and gastric disturbance; these signs may indicate that the baby is anxious and tense, distressed and fearful (Young Minds, 2003). Researchers suggest that these emotions need to be responded to with love and empathy by those on whom they depend for survival (Dwivedi and Harper, 2004).

As with adults, mental illness in children is diagnosed by noting signs and symptoms that suggest a particular disorder. Behaviours become symptoms when they occur very often, last a long time, occur at an unusual age or cause significant disruption to the child's and or the family's ability to function. First physical illness must be ruled out by the child's doctor, and then depending on the child's symptoms the illness is classified or diagnosed in order that a treatment programme can be planned. Outlined briefly below are some common classifications of children's mental health problems (please note this list is not exhaustive).

Separation anxiety disorder/anxiety disorders – inappropriate and excessive anxiety concerning separation from home or from those whom the child is attached (attachment difficulties). Children with anxiety disorders respond to certain things or situations with fear and dread as well as with physical signs of anxiety or nervousness such as rapid heart beat and sweating (panic or phobic disorders).

Attention deficit and disruptive behaviour disorders – children with these disorders tend to defy rules and often are disruptive in structured environments such as school. Behaviours related to inattention that are maladaptive (attention deficit or hyperactivity disorder); violation of the basic rights of others (conduct disorders or oppositional defiant disorder).

Pervasive development disorders – children with these disorders are confused in their thinking and generally have problems understanding the world around them (autistic disorders).

Feeding and eating disorders of infancy and early childhood – these involve intense emotions and attitudes as well as unusual behaviours associated with food and or weight.

Elimination disorders – these affect behaviour related to the elimination of body waste – faeces (encopresis) and urine (enuresis).

Tic disorders – these disorders cause a person to perform and repeat sudden involuntary and often meaningless movements and sounds called tics (Tourettes disorder).

In order to treat the child psychological, social and educational aspects of the child's problems must be addressed (DOH, 2004). The child's psychiatrist, counsellor, child psychotherapist, educational and clinical psychologists, social workers and other professional workers work together to formulate a treatment package that emphasizes evidence-based treatments that aim to provide a flexible individualized service tailored to the unique needs of the child and their family (Carr, 2000). The treatment approaches vary. Medication can be used and is effective with some childhood mental health problems. Psychotherapy which can include cognitive behavioural therapy; group therapy or family therapy may be used to address emotional responses to the mental illness. Creative therapies such as art therapy or play therapy may be helpful especially with the child who has trouble communicating thoughts and feelings. In many cases a successful treatment intervention will ensure that the distressing and disabling effects of mental illness can be minimized and ultimately prevented.

SUMMARY

This chapter has provided an overview of the activities involved in promoting child physical and mental health. It stresses the importance of a holistic approach to working with children and their families. A range of health professional roles are considered in trying to encompass three main health targets:

- promoting health and development
- identification of defects and disorders
- a public health approach to prevention and community development.

A variety of skills and a wide range of activities are undertaken to promote the health of children. Central to this work is the need to support parents. This is often achieved through early intervention, home-visiting programmes and 'parenting programmes' being incorporated into primary care delivery.

QUESTIONS FOR REFLECTION AND DISCUSSION

1. How can we provide children with the skills they need to be confident about leading a healthy lifestyle?

2. How can we promote an understanding of the full range of issues and behaviours which impact upon lifelong health?

3. What role do you play in promoting immunization?

4. Do you regard physical activity as a vital part of the curriculum and provide a range of options?

5. Why has children's mental well-being only recently received attention?

Recommended reading

Department of Health (2004) *National Service Framework for Children, Young People and Maternity Services*. London: HMSO.

Dwivedi, K.N. and Harper, B.P. (2004) *Promoting the Emotional Well Being of Children and Adolescents and Preventing their Mental Ill Health: A Handbook*. London: Jessica Kingsley.

Hall, D. and Elliman, D. (2004) *Health For All Children* (4th edn). Oxford: Oxford University Press.

Young Minds (2003) *Tuning in to Our Babies: The Importance of the Relationship Between Parents and Their Babies and Toddlers*. London: Young Minds.

Chapter 7

Children's learning

Tim Waller and Ros Swann

This chapter will focus on how children learn. The chapter provides a brief overview of traditional theories of learning and then considers learning relationships and dispositions in detail. In particular, the chapter will discuss a synopsis of recent theories of learning from a social constructive perspective including the work of Carr, Rogoff and Vygotsky. How children's play and sensitive adult interaction and 'scaffolding' support can contribute to successful learning is examined. Relationships, especially those with parents/carers, are seen as crucial to both learning and the general well-being of children. The chapter argues that modern learning theory has significant implications for early years pedagogy and learning in school.

This chapter provides an introduction to theories of learning, which is defined as how children make sense of reality and make meaning in a social world. The chapter briefly considers well-known models of learning that focus on individual construction of knowledge (Skinner and Piaget) and then discusses more fully the view of the child as an active co-constructor of knowledge (Bruner, Carr, Donaldson, Laevers, Lave Rogoff, Vygotsky, etc.). The chapter also discusses recent literature on learning relationships, dispositions, play and outdoor learning. Learning is considered generally, not in terms of school curricula (see BERA SIG, 2003; Siraj-Blatchford, 2004). However, the ideas about learning introduced in this chapter do have implications for learning and teaching in schools and readers are encouraged to reflect on this afterwards. Also, there is not scope within the chapter to give a detailed consideration of how children learn language, but it should be remembered that most children in the world are bilingual or multilingual (over 70 per cent). The ability to understand and speak more than one language can be a considerable benefit to learning in general (see Brown, 1998; Gregory, 1996; Riley, 2003).

Learning can be defined in a relatively straightforward way as the process of coming to know something, the acquisition of knowledge and skills. As Smidt (2002: 2) points out, in physiological terms learning can be very precisely demonstrated as when 'connections between cells are laid down and strengthened'. Bennett et al. (1984, cited in Moyles, 1997: 16), for example, offer a more extensive model. They put forward the view that learners demonstrate the ability to:

- acquire new knowledge and skills
- use existing knowledge and skills in different contexts
- recognize and solve problems
- practise what they know
- revise and replay what they know in order to retain it in the memory.

However, while acknowledging that learning leads to changes in understanding resulting in new knowledge and skills, recent literature and research in early childhood has focused on a wider view of learning involving context and relationships. As David (1999: 10) argues, learning is embedded in familiar contexts and on experience – it involves dispositions and relationships, including attitudes to learning and to oneself as a learner. Contemporary writing about learning has therefore highlighted the social nature of learning, viewing the child as an active and equal partner in the social process (Radford, 1999: 107, for example), but also recognizing the importance and significance of self-esteem (Laevers, 1994; Roberts, 2002, for example).

TRADITIONAL IDEAS ABOUT LEARNING

Most writing on childhood (for example, Kehily 2004: 5) identifies two central underlying themes that have influenced and continue to influence our view of the child and a child's learning. These ideas originated from philosophers writing during the 'Age of Enlightenment' in the late seventeenth and early to mid-eighteenth centuries (MacNaughton, 2003: 16). First, the Romantic view or discourse, influenced by the work of the French philosopher Rousseau (1712–78), claims that children are naturally innocent and pure, and only contaminated through exposure to the outside world. Rousseau believed that hurrying children into adult ways of thinking risks harming the child and that a young child under seven has a natural disposition to play that should be celebrated and protected. Second, the alternative discourse stems from the ideas of Locke (1632–1704) who argued that children are born as *tabula rosa*, 'blank slates' or empty vessels passively waiting to be educated and filled with 'knowledge' by adults. Childhood and learning in childhood is seen as essentially a period of preparation for adult life. From a contemporary perspective the significant weakness of both these views is that neither seem to allow the child any agency in her/his own learning. Also, they do not fully acknowledge the context of learning, learning relationships and relations of power between adults and children (Walkerdine, 1993; Silin, 1995, for example).

However, these underlying themes have an enduring influence on our understanding through 'commonsense' views, theories of child development and also on early years practice. Riley (2003: 15), for example, discusses how the Romantic view has led to a sentimental perspective of the child. As MacNaughton (2003: 17) points out, romantic beliefs are still popular as demonstrated by 'commonsense' views such as 'early experiences determine our future', 'the developing child is an incomplete adult and is different from adults' and 'we all progress through stages to adulthood'. Further, Locke's ideas still influence views of childhood through such examples as 'we can determine our own future', 'people of all ages learn in the same way' and 'effective learning is orderly and structured'. Despite their age and philosophical grounding, the theories of Rousseau and Locke had considerable influence over the supposedly 'scientific' understandings generated by developmental psychology. Woodhead (2003) has argued that in the early twentieth century developmental psychology became established as the dominant paradigm for studying children (see Chapter 5). Essentially this involved documenting the transitions and stages of western childhood (Kehily, 2004).

MacNaughton (2003: 15) argues that the maturationist view of Gesell is directly influenced by Romantic ideas of innocence and the important stimulus of nature. Gesell's view was that children progressed naturally towards adulthood through genetically pre-programmed structures. For example, early physical development frequently characterized as developing from sitting up (around 6 months), to crawling (6–9 months) and walking (12–15 months). However, the maturationist view does not fully acknowledge individual and cultural differences. Cultures around the world vary in how much and in what ways babies are carried about by adults or older children and this will impact on the sequence of physical development described above (see Smith and Cowie, 2003). Also, the behaviourist theories of Watson and Skinner were, for example, influenced by Locke (see Berk, 2000). Behaviourists believe that development is determined by the child's physical and social environment and that a child is more likely to repeat a behaviour if adults or the environment reinforce it. As MacNaughton (2003: 26) points out, behaviourism has had a powerful influence on child development and many early childhood educators' views of learning. Many child development books, especially those written in the USA are still from this perspective (see Chapter 5). However, as Hargreaves and Hargreaves (1997: 30) point out, behaviourist theory cannot fully explain more complex learning and behaviour that the child originates without apparent reinforcement, such as empathy, and the generation of language. A memorable example of this is provided by the author's daughter Amy when, aged three years and two months, she commented on a particularly heavy downpour in terms of:

'It's chuckling it down.'
'Do you mean chucking it down?'
'No it's chuckling it down because it's funny rain.'

MODERN IDEAS ABOUT LEARNING

This section now provides a brief overview of Piaget's work to acknowledge the significant impact and influence of his views. However, a detailed account is not given because his work is well known and there are many good sources of information about Piaget, such as Penn (2005), Riley (2003) and Arnold (2003). Attention is then concentrated on contemporary perspectives of the learning process.

Constructivism

Piaget focused on how children acquire knowledge. Piaget has had an enduring influence on our understanding of early learning (see Penn, 2005: 40, for an overview). For example, many early years practitioners in the UK have been influenced by Athey's work on children's 'schemas', which was derived from Piaget's ideas. 'Schemas are patterns of repeatable actions that lead to early categories and then logical classifications' (Athey, 1990: 36). Arnold (2003) provides an interesting discussion of the schemas exhibited over a number of years by one particular child (Harry).

It is also important to acknowledge that the results of many of Piaget's ingenious experiments have been challenged and disputed because they did not take into account the context of children's learning (see Donaldson, 1978). Donaldson (1978, 1993) emphasized the need for embedded learning – that is learning embedded in the context of meaningful experiences for children. When children are involved in tasks that are meaningful to them they achieve greater success. When children are involved in 'disembedded' tasks that are not meaningful the process of learning is significantly more difficult, as with many school-based tasks (1993: 19).

One of the most significant aspects of Piaget's work was the identification of stages on the way to becoming a logical thinker. For Piaget the child is an active enquirer trying to make sense of their world, constructing an intellectual map for themselves. Children gradually structure their minds, described by Piaget as a series of major changes or stages in development:

- The *sensori-motor* stage (0–2 years): learning is from and through physical (or motor) action
- The *pre-operational period* (3–7 years): learning in is intuitive in nature
- The *concrete operational* stage (8–11 years): learning is logical but depends on concrete referents (real experiences)
- *Formal operations* (12–15 years): learning and thinking involves abstractions, generalizing rules from experience.

As an example, Piaget's theory could be applied to the game of chess. In the sensori-motor phase the child would play with the pieces and in the pre-operational stage learn to move the pieces. During the concrete operational phase the moves and strategies would be learned from experience of playing and in the formal operations stage players are able to think several moves ahead and try to work out their opponent's strategy in advance. Of course, many children learn to play chess well before the age of 12, although Piaget did not see the stages as being fixed and static (see Smith and Cowie, 2003). While the stages of learning (or cognitive development) identified by Piaget are associated with characteristic age spans, they vary for every individual.

Piaget argued that learning consists of a constant effort to adapt to the environment in terms of *assimilation and accommodation*. Learning takes place through the processes of adaptation: assimilation and accommodation. Assimilation involves the interpretation of events in terms of existing cognitive structure, whereas accommodation refers to changing the cognitive structure to make sense of the environment. An example would be a six-month-old child playing with a beach ball. The child initially tries to put the ball in her mouth (as with most other things) and is unable to do so because the ball is too big. The child assimilates this knowledge and accommodates it by adapting her behaviour to lick the ball instead.

Following Piaget, Bruner (1990) also viewed learning an active process in which learners construct new ideas or concepts based on their current and past knowledge (see Hargreaves and Hargreaves, 1997). Drawing on the work of Piaget, he developed a theoretical framework that views learning as three increasingly powerful ways of representing the world:

- *Enactive representation*: thought based only on actions
- *Iconic representation*: child can form and use images of objects without the objects having to be present
- *Symbolic representation*: child can use and think in terms of symbols such as words.

For Bruner the learner selects and transforms information, constructs hypotheses, and makes decisions, relying on a cognitive structure or framework to do so. This mental model provides meaning and organization to experiences and allows the individual to 'go beyond the information given'.

Multiple intelligence

Gardner (1983) argued that people learn in different ways and that there are different types of intelligences. He suggested that everyone possesses each type of intelligence to varying degrees. Gardner identified the following seven different types of intelligence:

- bodily-kinaesthetic
- linguistic

- logical and mathematical
- musical
- visual and spatial
- social (inter-personal)
- personal (intra-personal).

A key element of Gardner's theory is that learning and intelligence is not fixed. It can and does change throughout each individual's lifetime. Measuring only one aspect of intelligence, such as a single IQ measurement is therefore meaningless. As Gardner (1983: 70) points out 'these intelligences are fictions and most useful fictions – for discussing processes and abilities that (like all of life) are continuous with one another'. Gardner is critical of schooling because he feels that it recognizes and promotes a limited view of intelligence (especially logical-mathematical). One of the strengths of his theory is that multiple intelligence draws attention to the uniqueness of the learning of each individual child and recognizes the culturally diverse patterns of learning. As Penn (2005: 54) points out:

> It is clear that in different societies different kinds of intelligence are valued. Euro-American societies (over) value linguistic and logico-mathematical intelligence. Other societies, for instance some communities in northern India or West Africa may value musical and kinaesthetic intelligence very highly – for example the praise singers of Mali and Senegal.

Metacognition

Metacognition is 'thinking about thinking', it involves children's ability to reflect on their own thinking and learning. This aspect of learning has recently received greater attention and Brown (1987), for example, shows how metacognitive experiences involve the use of strategies or regulation. They include knowledge about the nature of a task as well as the type of demands that the task will place upon the individual. These processes help to regulate and oversee learning, and consist of planning and monitoring cognitive activities, as well as checking the outcomes of those activities. As David (1999: 5) rightly points out, children under the age of seven are unlikely to have fully developed mental strategies such as rehearsal and organizing their thoughts and will develop these through adult modelling and scaffolding (see below). The point about metacognition is that it does not suddenly develop in later childhood, it is founded in early learning relationships. For example, Hudson (1993) discusses the scripts and scenarios that children use to inform themselves about a particular experience. Children have to learn these in order to know how to act in different social situations. They learn what behaviour is expected of them and can predict what others are likely to do (see Merry, 1997).

Clearly, children will hold views about their success as learners. Dweck and Leggett (1998) conducted research into the views children hold about their approach to learning. They identified two possible learning dispositions: 'mastery' (where children approached new tasks enthusiastically, were determined to succeed and took responsibility for their learning) and 'helpless' (where children showed little interest in new tasks, gave up easily and tended to rely on others to help them). Dweck and Leggett emphasize the importance of 'mastery' learning dispositions in children (see below for further discussion on dispositions).

Social constructivism

For Rogoff (1997: 269) 'learning' is a process of improving one's participation in systems of activity, particularly social systems:

> From a socio-cultural perspective, developmental processes are not just within individuals but also within group and community processes. Hence individual children are not regarded as developing with everything else static.

This is a view that gives much greater recognition to the importance of social interaction and support for the learner than Piaget's 'lone scientist' (1954) and proposes the learner as a social constructor of knowledge. Vygotsky (1978) asserted that a group working together can construct knowledge to a higher degree than can individuals in that group working separately. The knowledge is dependent upon the group interaction. Individuals working alongside more knowledgeable others can 'borrow' their understanding of tasks and ideas to enable them to work successfully (see Wray and Medwell, 1998: 8). For example, consider how a parent/carer may support a child's early literacy development during a 'bedtime story'. Importantly, the context is one where the child is comfortable and expects to succeed. For Rogoff (1990: vii) 'children's cognitive development is an apprenticeship – it occurs through guided participation in social activity with companions who support and stretch children's understanding of and skill in using the tools of culture'.

Scaffolding

Wood et al. (1976) were first to use the term 'scaffolding' as a metaphor for the process by which an adult assists a child to carry out a task beyond the child's individual capability. Through the process of 'scaffolding', the adult guides and supports the child's learning by building on what the child is able to do (Wood et al., 1976; Bruner, 1978; Wells, 1987; Tharp and Gallimore, 1991). Bruner (1978) links 'scaffolding' explicitly with Vygotsky's concept of the 'zone of proximal development' (ZPD). ZPD is Vygotsky's model for the mechanism through which social interaction facilitates cognitive development. It resembles an apprenticeship in which a novice works closely with an expert in joint problem solving in the zone of proximal development (ZPD). The novice is thereby able to participate in skills beyond those that she or he is independently capable of handling.

Originally, little attention was paid to the means by which the transfer of responsibility from the adult to the child was accomplished. However, more recent discussions of the term scaffolding have shifted from an emphasis on relations in which the adult is directing to an emphasis on mutuality (Stone, 1998). Mutuality describes the degree of emotional intimacy and intuitive understanding involved in 'joint activities'. It concerns the way in which adult utterances tend to respond directly to, and to extend, the communicative intent of the children. What the adult does and says in these situations is therefore based on, and responsive to, the state of understanding achieved by the child (Lepper et al., 1997).

Rogoff (1998: 698) criticises the specific linking of ZPD with scaffolding because much of the early writing and research about scaffolding located the power and control with the adult. Berk and Winsler (1995) develop a conception of scaffolding where there is a focus on joint problem solving and inter-subjectivity. They assert that: 'inter-subjectivity creates common ground for communication as each partner adjusts to the perspective of the other' (1995: 27). As Jordan (2004: 33) points out, Rogoff (1998) distinguishes between the function of scaffolding where an expert assists a child and ZPD where participants mutually contribute to learning.

Jordan (2004: 32) discusses a significant difference between scaffolding, where the adult or teacher is seen as an expert ànd co-construction, where there is equal partnership between the adult and child. The emphasis in co-construction is on the child as a powerful player in his/her own learning. The partnership between adults and children therefore focuses on forming meaning and building knowledge with each other. Jordan argues that when children are involved in co-construction they become full members of their communities of learning through accepting greater responsibility for their own learning (Wenger, 1998). Rogoff (1998: 690) described this as a 'transformation of participation'. She identifies three interwoven levels or planes – the personal, the interpersonal and the community/institutional as sites for this transformation. For Rogoff development is 'a process of transformation of participation where individuals participate and contribute to ongoing activity' (1998: 695). Learning and development are therefore inseparable from the concerns of families and interpersonal and community processes.

Learning as a relationship and a disposition

The relationships children develop with their mother and 'significant other' people, including family and friends and themselves, form the basis of their social world and are extremely significant in shaping and supporting their learning. Bruner (1986) argued that most learning in most settings is a communal activity – a sharing of the culture. As Anning and Edwards (1999: 63) point out, the learning path followed by many children from birth to eight is one of gradual shift from interdependence to independence, from a focus on personal meanings to public meanings. In many western childhoods this means moving from family and community to early years setting and formal schooling.

Trevarthen (1977) conducted research with infants of only a few weeks old and identified a sharing, democratic character of early interactions between children and parents. Gopnik et al. (1999: 32) also argue that 'babies understand that there is something special about other people and that they are linked to other people in a special way'. Trevathen's concept of 'motherese' is important here as the rhythm and melody of the mother's voice helps to encourage a partnership of shared interest (see Arnold, 2003: 70). Rogoff (1990: 12) also acknowledges the value of parental involvement: 'parents routinely adjust their interaction and structure children's environments in ways consistent with providing support for learning'.

This 'intersubjectivity' is crucial to learning for two significant reasons. First 'the child is using other people to figure out the world' (Gopnik et al., 1999: 34). Second it is in this physical and psychological space between participants that the participants develop strategies to tune into each other (Trevarthen, 1993) and the disposition to learn (see Anning and Edwards, 1999: 64).

For Schaffer (1992), learning occurs through interactions with objects. Objects may be used in different ways in different communities. Schaffer (1992) paid particular attention to the 'joint involvement episodes' where adults and children play joint attention to and act on an object. In these everyday exchanges the quality of the interaction influences the quality of learning. The variable quality of interaction between children and adults was evident in a study by Tizard and Hughes (1984). They recorded the conversations of 30 four-year-old girls with their mothers at home and their nursery teachers at school. Their findings suggested that children's learning was significantly more useful and challenging at home because it was embedded in meaningful contexts and involved conversations initiated by the child.

The Effective Provision of Pre-school Education (EPPE) research in the UK has identified a range of practice in early years settings that has a strong influence on children's learning. In settings which were assessed as 'excellent', children and adults were more likely to be involved in 'sustained shared thinking'. According to Siraj-Blatchford (2004: 147) sustained shared thinking involves 'episodes in which two or more individuals "worked together" in an intellectual way to solve a problem, clarify a concept, evaluate activities or extend narratives, etc. During a period of sustained shared thinking both parties contributed to the thinking and developed and extended the discourse.'

Friendship

Children's learning is also increasingly influenced by their friendships – especially when they start school (see Brooker, 2002). Hartup (1996) describes friendship as a close association, leading to psychological attachment and trust. It is an affiliation between equals. Hartup (1996) argues that friendships serve as contexts for acquiring social skills, information about the world and cognitive and emotional resources. Children with friends are more likely to be socially competent than those who are not.

Dunn et al. (1987) observed and analysed the conversations of three and four-year-old children with their mothers, siblings and friends. They argued that children with more advanced understanding of other people's minds were more likely to have:

- engaged in pretend play more when they were two years old
- more connected interactions between friends at age three
- taken part in conversations about why people behave as they do
- witnessed an intense relationship between two other family members.

Pollard (1996) conducted an extensive study on the social world of five children's learning, based around the first years of schooling. A range of evidence from the children's social lives was collected from family, friends and teachers. As a result of his study Pollard argued that children who learned most effectively were able to manage their classroom identities so that they derived support from both teachers and peers.

Self-esteem

Self-esteem is linked to self-concept, it relates to how children see themselves and how they behave as a result of their self-perception. As Schaffer (1996: 159) points out self-concept derives from experience which if perceived as successful generates feelings of competence, and if perceived as unsuccessful generates feelings of incompetence. Roberts (1998: 161) argues that, 'children's self-esteem is a key factor not only for their well-being but also for learning outcomes'. However, self-esteem is a complex concept. Brooker and Broadbent (2003: 33) make an important point about the self-esteem of young children:

> Self-esteem has been described as the value that a child assigns him or herself: attempts to measure or describe it have focused on the disparity between what a child would like to be like and that child's view of how he or she actually is. But in early childhood it principally reflects the value the child perceives he or she has in the eyes of others, particularly those 'significant others' whose opinions count most.

Curry and Johnson (1990: 5–9, cited in Roberts 2002: 12) identify four areas of self-esteem:

1 Acceptance (between mother and child and other significant people including family and friends).
2 Control (exerting control over environment and self-control).
3 Moral worth (developing concept of good and bad, right and wrong).
4 Competence (ability to solve problems and resulting sense of competence).

Roberts (2002: 105) argues that the characteristic of acceptance is at the core of self-concept and that 'unconditional acceptance' is critical for self-esteem. She defines unconditional acceptance as 'the sort of acceptance that babies need from parents and other important people is acceptance that is independent of behaviour; without reservations and without judgements' (Roberts, 2002: 5). Further, Roberts (2002: 105) identifies the components of self-esteem, in particular 'high self-esteem' as:

● positive self-concept (secure sense of identity)
● confidence, energy and optimism
● positive experiences.

Dispositions

How a child learns is seen as equally important as what she learns (Riley, 2003: 17). Self-esteem clearly influences learning dispositions. As Anning and Edwards (1999: 63) point out, 'dispositions are rooted in our sense of our likely effectiveness'. Katz (1995: 62) defines dispositions as 'relatively enduring habits of mind or characteristic ways of responding to experience across different types of situations'. Research on learning dispositions suggests that fostering positive dispositions leads to children becoming more purposeful, successful and less likely to become disaffected (Brooker and Broadbent, 2003: 51). For Katz (1995: 63) some dispositions to learn (such as exploration) are inborn but these can be adversely affected and even destroyed by inappropriate learning experiences. Dispositions are learnt through early experience. High quality early learning involves supporting and strengthening learning dispositions (Sylva, 1994; Carr, 2001).

Laevers (1994) argue that when children are engaged in 'deep level learning' they have a positive disposition, which is displayed through high levels of 'well-being' and 'involvement'. Well-being is described as 'feeling at home, being oneself and feeling happy'. Involvement concerns 'the intensity of the activity, the extent to which one is absorbed, to find pleasure in exploration' (Laevers, 1994: 5). The two dispositions are closely linked and, according to Laevers (1994) are indicated by a number of signs. Well-being is indicated by the following:

- openness and receptivity
- flexibility
- self-confidence and self-esteem
- assertiveness
- vitality
- relaxation and inner peace
- enjoyment without restraint
- being in touch with one's self.

Signs of involvement include:

- concentration
- complexity and creativity
- persistence
- reaction time
- satisfaction
- energy
- facial expression and composure
- precision
- verbal expression.

Laevers developed a five-point scale to assess children's well-being and involvement levels (see Arnold, 2003: 32).

Carr (2001) views learning dispositions as situated in and interwoven with action and activity, not as an individual attribute like temperament. For Carr (2001: 21) learning dispositions are 'situated learning strategies plus motivation – participation repertoires from which a learner selects, edits, responds to, searches for and constructs learning opportunities'. Carr (2001: 21) cites Katz (1988: 30) who argues that, 'dispositions are a very different type of learning from skills and knowledge. They can be thought of as habits of mind, tendencies to respond to situations in certain ways.'

Carr (2001: 23) identifies five domains of learning disposition as:

1 taking an interest
2 being involved
3 persisting with difficulty
4 communicating with others
5 taking responsibility.

Carr (2001: 23) analysed these domains in three parts: 'being *ready* (seeing oneself as a participating learner); being *willing* (evaluating opportunities for learning and being sensitive to them); being *able* (having funds of knowledge and skills to support being ready and will-ing). They involve a combination of inclination, sensitivity to occasion and the relevant skill and knowledge.'

Carr developed the five domains of learning disposition as a framework for assessing learning from multiple perspectives (including the child's perspective), which she termed 'learning stories'. 'Learning stories' are structured narrative documentation based on critical incidents of chil-dren's learning, including the child's own comments (see Carr, 2001: 96).

PLAY AND LEARNING

It is recognized that play is important for both children and adults. Play is recreative and gives individuals the opportunity to step outside the world of work and relax, or focus their attention on something different.

For young children, however, play is more than recreation, it is the foundation for all learning (Bruce, 2001; David, 1999; Moyles, 1994).

While the understanding that play is central to early learning is one of the fundamental principles of the care and education of young children in the UK, play is, in fact, hard to define. Perceptions of play and its importance in early cognitive development will depend very much on cultural and social constructs of children (BERA SIG, 2003; Curtis, 1994; Sayeed and Guerin, 2000).

Tamis-Lemonda, Katz and Bornstein (2002: 229, cited in Macleod-Brudenell, 2004: 213) identify the significance of play in five areas of development:

1 *Psychological* – the regulation of arousal, expressing emotions, resolution of conflicts.
2 *Mastery* – developing attention span and task-directed behaviour.
3 *Cognitive* – the acquisition of information and skills, creative and divergent thinking, representational abilities.
4 *Social* – giving and receiving, taking account of others' thoughts and intentions in decision-making.
5 *Culture* – the means of transmitting social roles and cultural values.

Parten in 1932, (cited in Smith and Cowie 2003: 141) identified four stages of young children's play. The first stage is described as solitary play in which children play on their own, though more recent research suggests that fantasy or pretend play is often more social than was first recognized. The second stage of play is parallel play in which children will play alongside each other and interact with one another but may not necessarily be involved in one another's play. The third stage is associative play in which children may interact with one another and involve themselves in each other's play. The fourth stage is co-operative or collaborative play, in which children are involved in each other's play and work together to achieve a common goal.

Corinne Hutt (1966) defined play as falling into three categories: Epistemic play which is characterized as knowledge based, Ludic play, characterized as symbolic, representative and fantasy-based and Games with Rules (see Figure 7.1).

Figure 7.1 Categories of play

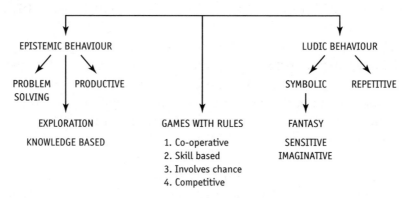

Source: Hutt, 1966

All aspects of play, however, will provide opportunities for developing skills and understanding in all areas of development. Ludic play, for example, can involve children in problem solving, developing language skills, empathy and collaborative skills. In addition, when we observe children playing, for example, in socio-dramatic or role play, we can see that they are drawing on the knowledge they already have:

> In the urge to explain and categorise play, we may be in danger of overlooking the fact that children define play themselves. They often establish mutual awareness of play and non-play situations. They create roles, use symbols, redefine objects, and determine the action through negotiation and shared meanings ... play is not just about fantasy. It doesn't have a life of its own which is divorced from reality. Children continuously weave in and out of their play their knowledge and understanding gleaned in other areas of their lives.
>
> (Wood and Attfield, 1996: 85)

While there are often generally agreed features that we use to describe play, these are not always consistent characteristics. For example, play is often described as active, but this is not always the case as play can involve apparent inactivity. Play or playfulness can be identified though by a number of different criteria, one of the most significant being that it is self-chosen.

Throughout history many theorists have discussed the purpose of play in children's lives. It can be seen that all young animals play and it is clear how the lion or bear cub is practising those skills that it will need to survive in adulthood. For the human baby though, life will be far more complex, and the relationship between play and early learning is less clear-cut.

Theorists such as Friedrich Froebel writing in 1906 believed that play developed from within the child but could be encouraged and developed by adults with the provision of appropriate materials.

Maria Montessori (1976), whose work has had a great influence on practice in pre-school settings, also believed in the importance of play and like Froebel, considered that play should be structured by adults, giving children the opportunity to learn real life skills. Both Montessori and Froebel did not really recognize the importance of fantasy and role-play in children's learning. The principle of respecting the child's choice is, however, central to practice in Montessori settings.

Piaget (1952, see Smith and Cowie, 2003) believed that play consolidates pre-existing skills by providing the opportunity for rehearsing them and that it gave the children a sense of mastery over an action that resulted in increased confidence. He believed that during play children are given the opportunity to test themselves without the fear of failing.

Sigmund Freud believed that play gave children the opportunity to act out sometimes 'dangerous' desires in that it could provide a safe context in which children could express their feelings without fear of punishment. He also recognized that play can help children and overcome traumatic events in their lives.

Susan Isaacs, writing in 1929, believed in the fundamental importance of play in children's lives for both cognitive and social/emotional development. 'Play is indeed the child's work, and the means whereby he grows and develops. Active play can be looked upon as a sign of mental health; and its absence either some form of inborn defect, or of mental illness' (cited in Smith and Cowie, 2003: 231).

Like Susan Isaacs, Lev Vygotsky (1933: 231) recognized the significance of play in both children's cognitive and emotional development. He believed, as Freud did, that children played out their 'unrealisable desires' but in a more general sense. Unlike Montessori and Froebel,

Vygotsky also recognized the importance of fantasy or pretend play in young children's development. He suggested that because pretend play released children from the constraints of more formal learning, they were able to operate and think at a more sophisticated level.

The centrality of play in the early years curriculum has long been, and still is, the subject of much debate both in political and educational contexts. Early years practitioners and theorists, particularly those concerned with pre-school settings, have defended the role of play since the late 19th and 20th centuries and the principles of play-based learning are now enshrined in the Foundation Stage document (DFEE, 2000).

Much of the argument has been based on a common sense understanding of how young children learn and early laboratory-based studies. Hutt (1966) and Smith (1978) provided little evidence as to the cognitive gains that children could make though play. They did concede, however, that children's social development was enhanced through play. The connection between social play and children's cognitive development was not made at this time.

More recent observational studies (Nutbrown, 1994) have given us greater insights into how children's social and cognitive development takes place during play and social constructivist theories such as those of Vygotsky (1933, see Smith and Cowie, 2003) have reinforced our understanding of the importance of play. In addition, recent neuro-science research on brain development in young babies (Perry, 1996 in Mustard and MaCain, 1999) confirm the essential role of play in aiding the forming of neuron synapse connections in the brain and the impact of the emotions on cognitive development is now more clearly understood (see Chapter 5).

It is recognized that young children are active learners (minds as well as bodies) who find it easier to learn through concrete experiences and materials and for whom a simple transmission model of teaching is inappropriate (Donaldson, 1978). It is also known that young children are powerful if inexperienced learners who will need both the skills and tools for learning that they can access through play (Bruce, 2001). It is important to remember, though, that as well as providing the opportunity to develop those skills, play provides the context in which children can develop the dispositions of perseverance, collaboration, problem solving, responsibility and independence.

OUTDOOR LEARNING

Bailey et al. (2003: 176) argue that outdoor play holds a special place in the education of young children, offering countless experiences that contribute to healthy development. For Lasenby (1990: 5) the outdoor environment is an integral part of early years provision and ideally should be available to children all the time. Bilton (1999), for example, acknowledges that outdoor activity is integral to the whole learning environment. In addition, some children are socially inhibited in indoor environments.

However, Rickinson et al. (2003) conducted a review of research on outdoor learning and found, as Fjørtoft (2001), there has been relatively little research on how the natural environment functions as a playground for young children, and even less is known about what effects such a playground may have on learning in children. Even in Scandinavia, where it is common for many kindergartens to include the outdoor environment in curriculum, relatively few studies have been undertaken in this field.

The studies by Fjørtoft (2001) and Rickinson et al. (2003) indicate that playing in the natural environment seems to have positive effects on children, they become more creative in their play, play activities increase and children's motor fitness improves. Fjørtoft (2001) demonstrated that young children using the diverse natural landscape of the forest as a playscape performed better in motor skills than children used to traditional playgrounds. In particular, she found that significant improvements were made in balance and co-ordination activities. Fjørtoft and Sageie (2000) studied the use of the forest as a supplement to the kindergarten by children aged 5, 6 and 7, suggesting multivariable possibilities for versatile play and a strong relationship between landscape structures and play functions. Despite these valuable insights there is clearly a need for much further research into the outdoor experiences of young children in both educational settings and at home (see BERA SIG, 2003; Waller et al., 2004).

SUMMARY

Children learn through interaction with other people and the environment, in an appropriate social context that offers support, scaffolding and encouragement. They learn through and with their mother, family and friends. Learning disposition, including self-esteem, attitudes and feelings is an extremely significant aspect of learning. As Merry (1997: 60) states, this is 'because successful problem solving requires not only appropriate strategies, but also positive attitudes towards the problem and yourself as a learner and a problem solver'.

Following Merry (1997: 60) and Roberts (2002: 89) the characteristics of successful learners can be summarized as follows:

- high self-esteem
- see themselves as good learners
- expect to succeed
- seek a challenge
- are prepared to take risks
- persevere and have an 'internal locus of control'.

Learning is complex, but children are actively engaged in problem solving of their own making from birth. They are trying to make sense of, and participate in, their social world and it is important not to underestimate children's ability to understand.

QUESTIONS FOR REFLECTION AND DISCUSSION

1. How do the views of Piaget and Rogoff differ in relation to children's learning?
2. Can you think of any aspects of children's learning that may be naturally scaffolded by parents/carers?
3. Can you think of particular activities where children benefit from supporting each other's learning?
4. Why are relationships seen as so important to learning?
5. Is there a difference between learning in school and learning outside school?
6. Why is this?
7. What are the implications of your discussion for teaching and learning in early years settings and schools?

Recommended reading

Arnold, C. (2003) *Observing Harry: Child Development and Learning 0–5*. Maidenhead: Open University Press.

British Educational Research Association Early Years Special Interest Group (BERA SIG) (2003) *Early Years Research: Pedagogy, Curriculum and Adult Roles, Training and Professionalism*. Southwell, Notts: BERA.

Bilton, H. (1999) *Outdoor Play in the Early Years: Management and Innovation*. London: David Fulton.

Brooker, L. and Broadbent, L. (2003) 'Personal, social and emotional development: the child makes meaning in the world', in J. Riley (ed.) *Learning in the Early Years: A Guide for Teachers of 3–7*. London: Paul Chapman Publishing. pp. 29–60.

Carr, M. (2001) *Assessment in Early Childhood Settings*. London: Paul Chapman Publishing.

Moyles, J.R. (1994) *The Excellence of Play*. Buckingham: Open University Press.

Roberts, R. (2002) *Self-esteem and Early Learning*. London: Paul Chapman Publishing.

Sayeed, Z. and Guerin, E. (2000) *Early Years Play: A Happy Medium for Assessment and Intervention*. London: David Foulton.

Useful websites

trackstar.hprtec.org (general information on Piaget, Bruner and Vygotsky)

www.psyc.bbk.ac.uk (Centre for Brain and Cognitive Development Research)

tip.psychology.org/vygotsky (overview of Vygotsky's ideas)

Chapter 8

Studying children

Jane Murray

This chapter examines the contexts and rationales of the study of children in contemporary western society. It explores four major components of the study of children:

- observation
- dialogue
- agency
- making professional judgements.

The chapter continues with exploration and discussion of the following areas:

- domains in which children are studied
- construction of childhood, in the context of the study of children
- why study children
- child study by health care, social care and education practitioners.

In conclusion, the chapter offers questions for reflection and a short recommended reading list for practitioners wishing to explore further practical features of child study.

> It takes a whole village to bring up a child.
>
> African Proverb

This section will explore different reasons and models for studying children and for what and whom that study is in place. Nutbrown (1999: 127) hints that this area is complex as she offers three purposes for the assessment of children:

1 Teaching and learning.

2 Management and accountability.

3 Research.

Although grounded in the work of early years' settings, the rubric is a useful indicator demonstrating that children may be scrutinized more widely for a range of different reasons. In identifying four audiences as recipients of assessment documentation: community agencies, families, practitioners and children, Carr (2001: 126) appears to support Nutbrown's notion of the complex nature of the study of children and in developing this further, it can be argued that this complexity requires that several components come together to achieve the whole picture. It may further be argued that these components might include observation, dialogue, agency and professional judgement. In terms of effective early years practice, Nutbrown (1996: 55) draws together the four components, explaining that: 'Adults with expertise who respectfully watch children engaged in their process of living, learning, loving and being are in a better position to understand what it is these youngest citizens are trying to say and find ways of helping them to say it.'

In order to gain a fuller understanding of the four components, it is helpful to explore each in more depth.

OBSERVATION

Nutbrown (2001: 66) describes observation as 'one of the best "tools of the trade"', in discussing the work of early years practitioners and if one accepts Bruce's 'Ten Bedrock Principles' (1997: 17) as a sound foundation for high quality early years practice, it is important to note that it is necessary to observe the child in order to establish many of them. However, this type of child study can be less straightforward than it might initially appear.

One example of this might be the nature of the technique used. While a universal schedule might appear to provide a framework for a 'fair test' for as many children as may be observed, it is important to consider the elements within that framework that may be open to deviation, for example:

- environment (time, place, antecedents)
- the mood, interactions and interests of the observed child
- the experience, background and personality of the observer.

Clearly, elements of each of these affect process and outcome of any observation, which must mean that it would be very difficult indeed to ensure that one observation is as fair a test as any other. For this reason, it is most important to ensure that any observer acknowledges the likely variants before, during and after any observation. This chapter concludes with recommended reading for practitioners involved in observation of children as part of their work.

DIALOGUE

When I began my teaching career with a class of 30 six-year-olds in 1983, I had received no training in how to develop and maintain a dialogue with primary carers or, indeed my colleagues. In fact, this barely mattered, since we had one very short annual meeting with parents and all the classrooms were completely separate from each other. Curricular freedom abounded in those days – there was no National Curriculum – and teachers frequently planned and worked unilaterally. In those days, there were very few adults other than teachers (AOTTs) working in classrooms; dialogue was reserved for break-time in the staff room! At the time in England, there was one major exception to this and that was the 1981 Education Act, which promoted a multiagency approach to supporting children with special educational needs (SEN). This proved to be a template for much that was to come later.

Current policy and practice encourages early years practitioners to discuss planning and implementation with a range of colleagues and from a range of agencies. Integrated children's services have clearly been identified by international bodies such as World Health Organisation (1999), United Nations Children's Fund (2003) and the United Nations Educational, Scientific and Cultural Organisation (2004) as highly desirable and, in England, multidisciplinary approaches have become legislation through the Children Acts of 1989 and 2004, with research such as that of Sylva et al. (2004) to support them.

Effective dialogue with parents has also been identified as a key indicator for children's effective learning and development and early years practitioners work hard to develop these relationships through effective, equal and long-lasting dialogue: 'Wise practitioners look to learn from the parents of the children they are trying to help' (Draper and Duffy, 2001: 149).

Dialogue between young children and practitioners that is equitable and respectful is a key learning tool for both children and practitioners and links to other areas of the study of children. As Cousins (1999: 28) observes: 'Listening to children and observing them go side by side' and indeed, Clarke and Moss (2001: 2) identified methods of doing precisely this in order to: 'Find practical ways to contribute to the development of services that are responsive to the "voice of the child" and which recognise children's competencies'. Jordan (2004: 31) additionally emphasizes this approach sited in early childhood centres in discussing 'dialogues with children in support of teaching and learning'.

Key to effective dialogue is that it leads to and emerges from the development and nurture of effective relationships: 'Relationships have been emphasised as central to the trajectory from early childhood experience into later learning' (Carr, 2001: 16), and the works of Catherwood (1999) and Gerhardt (2004) demonstrate the pivotal role of emotional development in later cognitive development.

AGENCY

As part of their work in supporting children to contribute to dialogue about issues affecting them directly, Clarke and Moss (2001) identify six domains in England where children's participation is becoming far more prevalent:

1 The law courts.
2 Research.
3 The arts.
4 Therapy and counselling.
5 Environment and community development.
6 Charities.

Clearly, international policy, such as the United Nations Convention on the Rights of the Child (1989) has affected national legislation (Children Acts, 1989, 2004) and this in turn is affecting practice. Schweinhart et al. (1993) offer an excellent rationale for children's agency in early years education and care and Scott describes what true agency might be like: 'Respecting children means finding out what they think and feel and responding honestly to their ideas and emotions' (1996: 43). Thus agency is somewhat of a *zeitgeist*, but the current emphasis upon self-advocacy is clearly rationalized by research and effective practice.

MAKING PROFESSIONAL JUDGEMENTS

The definition of effective professional judgement is not easy to make because early years workers bring so much of themselves to their work as Anning (2004b: 61) observes: 'Though it was possible to characterise the 20 professionals as coming from a specific tradition or work culture – welfare, education, health – their personal lives and work histories gave each practitioner a unique set of values and beliefs'.

Karstadt et al. assert that 'professionalism can be difficult to define' (2000: 26) and it follows that it must be difficult to know whether or not judgements based on that professionalism are 'right'. In looking at Figure 8.1 one observer may say: 'It is a vase', whereas another may say: 'It is two faces gazing at one another'.

Figure 8.1   A vase or a face?

The answer is open to individual interpretation: neither answer is right or wrong. The interpretation will depend upon the experiences that the observer brings to the observation. Equally, the children whom practitioners judge may well interpret the picture differently, dependant upon their experiences or personalities. Practitioners bring the sum of their personal and professional experiences to the judgements they make and, of course, this means that those judgements can never be wholly objective. However, subjectivity, or that which Eraut (1999, cited in Anning, 2004b: 64) terms 'P' (personal) knowledge can, as Eraut asserts, be diminished by combining it with that which he defines as 'C' (codified) knowledge, derived from reading the wealth of accumulated knowledge available from libraries and databases. For early years practitioners this often means combining knowledge of child development with that of individual children and within that there may exist an underlying tension between models of planning that precede children's actions and those which are responsive to those actions, by default following on from those actions. The practitioner must ask: 'In taking full account of the needs of young children, which should come first?' Centralized models tend to focus on planning as the first step, but in localized approaches, individual children's actions can be accounted for as part of the planning. This is because the more human scale of the localized approach can account for individual requirements as they differ and change. However, the latter approach is more complex and difficult to administer in comparison to the first and demands far more practitioner expertise and professional judgement.

In making judgements about young children's learning, development and welfare, it is crucial that practitioners recognize that every family has a different home culture. When early years practitioners study children, an evidence base is clearly most important (DoH, 2000). However, a limit to this exists and at that limit, the mark of a truly professional practitioner is that he or she acknowledges the inevitable bias in their judgements; bias can never be completely extinguished, since each of us is the sum of our parts. However, the explicit and considered reflection of this bias used together with an element of that which Manning-Morton and Thorp (2003: 155) term 'Instrumentality (thinking, rationality and logic)', may be the factors that turn judgements into professional judgements.

DOMAINS IN WHICH CHILDREN ARE STUDIED

In 21st century western society it is difficult not to observe children, since images of childhood invade our lives through a range of media. Whether we open magazines, turn on the television or read the newspaper, fascination with children is evident. For many years, advertisers have increasingly used and abused this fascination to make money for themselves and their clients. More recently, use of the worldwide web in the portrayal of children has become more prevalent (Holland, 2004), presenting a clear and present danger for children and childhood if adults' views and desired uses for images of children as, for example, sexual beings are displayed more extensively than ever before. The judgement used by the observer in this situation is likely to be subjective and primarily concerned with the observer's pleasure, not the nurture of the observed child. Possibly because of this, there is likely to be little or no dialogue between the observer and the observed, and little or no agency on the part of the observed child.

Another type of child study is evident in the data held by different local and national government departments. In Britain this derives from assessments of children's performance, health and welfare and, although much of it is used to detect trends, thereby enabling government departments to plan strategically, much is attributable to individual children, through, for example, each child's 'unique pupil number' (UPN), despite the existence of the Data Protection Act (1998) in Britain. As new data emerge, so another view of childhood is constructed, although that view is always tempered by the nature of the data commissioned. It may be argued that there is an underlying altruism in this type of child study, since it is a tool used by government to hold public services accountable for their actions, flagging up any ineffectiveness in service delivery; indeed, the Freedom of Information Act (Department for Constitutional Affairs, 2004) in Britain ensures that much of this type of data is available on demand. However, while observation and judgement are well used components of this type of child study, its large scale requires simplistic measurement, which significantly diminishes the likelihood of the human-scale elements of effective dialogue between the observer and the observed and any agency of either.

In addition to these purposes for the study of children there exists a clearly altruistic rationale for child study, evident in good early years practice in education, health and social care. High quality observations at a localized level enable practitioners, parents and the children themselves to gain a deep knowledge and understanding of individuals' development and learning. This is the type of study that incorporates observation by professionals who make time and space to know the child and his or her needs (Carr, 2001: 96–105; Scott, 2001: 21–29), who judge with an expert and nurturing eye (Athey, 1990; Bruce, 1997: 197–202; Nutbrown, 1999: 119; Edgington, 2004: 201), who work in partnership with primary carers (Willey, 2000: 92–100; Draper and Duffy, 2001: 146–153) and who involve children in developing their own futures (Carr, 2001: 180; Clarke and Moss, 2001; OfSTED, 2004a).

CONSTRUCTION OF CHILDHOOD AND THE STUDY OF CHILDREN

As discussed in Chapter 5, there exists a notion of childhood – indeed many childhoods – as social construction. Brooker (2002) and MacNaughton (2004) both subscribe to this. Many of the images of 'childhood' that saturate our lives today appear to damage any such positive perception of childhood's *construction*, and by default, effect a *destruction* of the social element that we call 'childhood'. This destruction seems to occur when children are *overpowered*, as opposed to *empowered* by adults, caused by 'the huge imbalance of power between adults and children' (Holland, 2004: 69). This imbalance of power can be used positively and counteracted, at least to some extent, by altruism. One expression of this is in United Nations Convention on the Rights of the Child (1989), as discussed in Chapter 1. A paradox within contemporary society emerges from these two paradigms. Children are widely observed as part of their exploitation; thus any notion of a protected childhood – at least for some – becomes damaged to the point of destruction. Simultaneously, developed global rhetoric monitors what is happening and advocates the safeguarding of childhood from that destruction.

Aligned with the latter – and contributing to a paradox at national level – English government is focused upon constructing one version of childhood. English policy for achieving this has been the National Childcare Strategy, launched in 1998 (DfES, 2004a). Millions of taxpayers' pounds have been spent to expand children's services, particularly in areas of socio-economic deprivation. Centralized frameworks for delivering and assessing children's experiences have included *Birth to Three Matters* (0–3 years) (DfES, 2004c) and *Curriculum Guidance for the Foundation Stage* (3–5 years) (DfEE, 2000). Additionally, assessment of all children in compulsory schooling in England is, of course, widespread and is publicly reported in league tables. Under the latest Office for Standards in Education (OfSTED) framework, the inspection body originally concerned with standards in schools and now also responsible for inspecting standards for all government funded childcare, the 'productivity' of the youngest children is judged (Ofsted, 2004b). A clear and less culturally diverse model of childhood is being constructed for the nation as millions of children receive similar learning experiences through *Birth to Three Matters* (DfES, 2004c), *Curriculum Guidance for the Foundation Stage* (DfEE, 2000), the National Curriculum (and accompanying approaches, such as the *National Literacy Strategy*) (DfEE, 1998) and the *National Numeracy Strategy* (DfEE, 1999). This mono-model is observed by practitioners, inspectors, parents, government, the public and, increasingly, the children themselves, as the move towards self-advocacy appears to gather pace (Claxton, 1990; Nutbrown, 1996; Cousins, 1999; Clarke and Moss, 2001; Carr, 2001; OfSTED, 2004c) supported by research such as that of Schweinhart (2001), Schweinhart et al. (1993) and Sylva et al. (2004).

There is no doubt that the simplistic mono-model of childhood is easy – and therefore cheap – to measure. It even appears easy to understand at first and is widely published for all to see. However, people are complex (Ryder and Wilson, 1997) and children are no exception. Therefore, it can be argued that a crude measure of a simplistic model of childhood may be inappropriate to the real needs of people. In fact, despite the growing rhetoric regarding the appropriateness of children's self-advocacy in all areas of their lives, children can hardly be said to be co-constructors of their own learning and development in a culture of centrally dictated curriculum and assessment. English government has made some concession to this with the Primary National Strategy, which appears to recognize the individualism of children and their needs (Leadbetter, 2004), but its maintained focus on publicized league tables seems to steer schools and, as an extension, children's services generally, towards a course for a culture of risk aversion.

WHY STUDY YOUNG CHILDREN?

Within both current paradigms of childhood – *destruction and construction* – the study of children is a central feature. Since this book is aimed at supporting the training of early childhood practitioners, the focus here will be on the rationale for the study of children as a tool to support the constructions of individual childhoods and in time, adulthoods, within cultures and a society built on positive values.

If one accepts central accountability as a fact of life in contemporary western society's culture relating to childhood services (Shuttleworth, 2003), but equally one accepts that a decentralized approach may be more appropriate to the learning needs of very young children (Moss and Petrie, 2003), the role of the practitioner is key in both answering to the paymaster, but also in preserving time and space for individual children to develop at a pace and in ways that are appropriate to them. Traditionally, early years practitioners have often compromised, perhaps because they have found it difficult to stand their ground in the face of hegemonic opposition frequently demonstrated by school leaders who do not fully understand the requirements of young children (Aubrey et al., 2002b) and Staggs acknowledges this issue: 'Many practitioners are intuitive ... they aren't very good at arguing their case' (in Palmer, 2004: 14). However, professional judgments based upon a multiple perspective evidence base of high quality observation, dialogue and child agency are likely to give practitioners a stronger voice in asserting their intuition in a professionally coherent manner. Athey (1990: 19) recognized the inevitability of this for teachers, but it can be argued that it is true for all early years' practitioners: 'Teachers need to advance their own theory and to become their own experts...to assist the process of accountability that requires an articulate rather than an intuitive professional knowledge'.

In addition to this, the study of children provides a window on their learning and development, but also an indicator for the next stages of that learning and development: the zone of proximal development (ZPD) (Vygotsky, 1978: 86–7), or what we are ready for next in our development (see Chapter 7). This is vital to the practitioner's ability to provide effectively for children's learning and development needs and is a strong rationale for all early years' practitioners to have a deep knowledge and understanding of child development.

Carr (2001: 20) uses the word 'surveillance' to describe that the onus on early years' practitioners in the role of assessors of children's development and learning could be less than positive. Certainly, this aligns with the accountability rationale for assessment of children. However, by suggesting another model, she empowers the practitioner: 'We have a responsibility to ensure that the new communities we are constructing for children ... are ethical and safe environments'.

Having established that the study of children is thrust upon the practitioner in the interests of accountability, the practitioner can work in an effective way to make that study work for the good of the children at its core. If 'ethical and safe' physical, social, emotional and intellectual space for children is to be created successfully, it needs to be done by the people who know the individual children best. These people are the children themselves and their primary carers, with practitioners working in close partnership as the professionals able to translate their requirements into reality. This partnership provides the dialogue and agency elements of child study, but it is the observation by the practitioner that joins these elements in a professional judgment to create a fuller picture of the child's development and learning status and the basis for future planning that will be used to enhance that status.

CHILD STUDY BY HEALTH PRACTITIONERS

Although Karstadt and Medd (2000: 72) point out that: 'All people working with young children should be aware of their health needs, being equipped to offer support and advice relating to child development', the World Health Organisation (1999) supports integrated services and in the UK the Department of Health (2004) endorses the importance of co-ordination in children's services, there is a clear and specific role for health practitioners in the UK.

Health practitioners screen unborn babies to ensure that their development is aligned with expected norms; ultrasound scanning is one widely used method and neonates are screened to establish the baby's ability for independent life using the 'Apgar Score' – a standardised assessment that provides a numerical measure for certain vital signs after birth. In addition to this, health practitioners assess baby health by checking physical features against norms. As children grow older, health screening continues, conducted by health visitors, practice and school nurses and general practitioners, so that it is highly unlikely that any condition outside the range of norms will remain undiagnosed by the time a child reaches compulsory school age. As a result, it is highly likely that children reaching compulsory school age conform to a fairly narrow range of physical norms, that they are moving towards that range with or without intervention, or that a decision has been made that they operate outside those norms with or without intervention.

It can be seen, therefore, that the work of health practitioners requires observation primarily. Dialogue takes place as part of the judgement evidence base for health practitioners, but in the case of child health screening this is predominantly with primary carers, since many of the very young children with whom they work are not yet old enough to consent in an informed way. As a result of this, agency for the very young service users of early years health practitioners may not be as great as the potential for the service users of other early years practitioners.

CASE STUDY

In her role as midwife, Sukinah was caring for Anna and new baby Sam on the maternity ward. Three days after Sam's birth, Sukinah observed that he had a significant yellow tinge to his skin. Sukinah was aware that in many neonates this is common because of physiological jaundice, caused by a build-up of bilirubin. This can cause serious neurological disorder. In Sam's case, Sukinah was particularly concerned because he was born at 37 weeks and she had observed that his weight had dropped by about 10 per cent since birth, despite the fact that he was feeding well. These factors can indicate a type of brain damage that causes cerebral palsy and hearing loss. Sukinah discussed the case with the doctor and a blood test and a phototherapy light to cover Sam's crib were arranged. The blood test indicated that there was no cause for concern and within two days, Sam's skin had lost its yellow hue, he had begun to gain weight and Sam and Anna were able to go home. Sukinah's careful observation, combined with her knowledge of physiological norms and possible outcomes of anomalies, enabled her to take a course of action that protected Sam from possible permanent neurological damage.

CHILD STUDY BY SOCIAL CARE PRACTITIONERS

Social workers not only observe as part of the assessment process, they also consult their service users, offering agency and engagement in dialogue in order to make judgements about aspects of children's lives to ensure their safety and nurture. However, the work that social care practitioners undertake in their study of children is different from that of health and education practitioners in that it is not universally applied to the population. The study of children by social care practitioners is likely to happen in response to a referral from another agency, for example, health, education or law, and is often preceded by concern for child safety. *The National Assessment Framework* (DoH, DfEE, Home Office, 2004) is the guidance for social care practitioners in the UK in this area of their work and recommends: 'A framework has been developed which provides a systematic way of analysing, understanding and recording what is happening to children and young people within their families and the wider context of the community in which they live. From such an understanding … clear professional judgments can be made'.

A particular feature of this type of child study, as distinct from child health screening for example, is that it is driven by individual need and therefore bespoke to each child. The gathering of a range of information from different sources is sought, thus providing a multiple perspective evidence base for greater reliability of judgment.

For the social care practitioner, a wide range of study techniques is suggested by the National Assessment Framework (DoH, 2000) and the child and his or her situation may be studied directly or indirectly. In the direct model, the child can become an advocate for his or her own future, by being given the agency to disclose his or her history and conduct dialogue about it in a safe environment. The Assessment Framework suggests that, in addition to this, indirect child study by social care practitioners might include working with parents, the family and other caregivers and locating other sources of knowledge, such as any other agencies with whom the family and child has had contact. Observation in a range of situations is also suggested as a key tool for the social care practitioner.

CASE STUDY

Michael, a social worker, visited siblings Rita (aged 8) and Adel (aged 7) at their foster family's home, with the intention of establishing their care experience and where they would like to live in the future. When working with the family in their own home, Michael established that their mother was in a violent relationship and that the children had been neglected. Michael witnessed this neglect in the children's dirty clothes, untreated lice in their hair and empty cupboards in the kitchen. On one occasion, neighbours had reported finding Adel and Rita sobbing on their doorstep at three o'clock one morning, while their mother was out with her boyfriend. Michael has spent time with the children's mother during the past few weeks and knows that she is desperate for the children to return. Michael has also visited the children's school where the headteacher reported that the children appear, for the first time, to be making appropriate progress with their schoolwork. Michael listens to the children say that, despite being happy at their foster home, they would like to return to live with their mother. He ensures that they are aware of the reasons why they had been placed in the foster home and makes a report for the court that advocates that the children may return once it has been established that they will be safe and nurtured by their mother who must demonstrate that she no longer has any contact with the violent boyfriend. Michael's careful direct and indirect observation establishes a holistic view of the children's situation that will enable their safety, care and happiness to be of prime consideration.

CHILD STUDY BY EDUCATION PRACTITIONERS

Both *Birth to Three Matters* (DfES, 2004c) and *The Curriculum Guidance for the Foundation Stage* (DfEE, 2000) advocate the study of children as a positive tool for supporting their learning and development. These documents prevail in early years settings in England and both frameworks advocate the practitioner's role in observing children's learning and development as key to further learning and development. Therefore, observation for learning and teaching is commonplace throughout England.

However, as discussed previously, this appears to be a much wider phenomenon. The global emphasis on accountability (Shuttleworth, 2003), provides a summative focus on what children have learned, as opposed to a diagnostic focus that leads into children's future learning and development. This may have the detrimental effect of diminishing the process and content of what children are learning, how they are learning and what it might be appropriate for them to learn in the future (Laevers, 2000). Indeed, Holland (2004: 76) notes: 'When testing and grading are all important, it is not learning, but the display of learning that counts', and Athey (1990: 19) asserts the impact of the accountability at school level: 'The delivery of the curriculum and formative evaluation of what children have actually received from what is offered will remain the central concerns of the teacher'.

Nutbrown (1999: 128) argues that 'respect for children' is a 'feature of effective early assessment' and it is questionable whether accountability as a purpose for assessment offers respect for children – it is more likely to offer respect for adults and even more likely to offer it for money, or both in a culture of payment by results. If one accepts Nutbrown's assertion, it is possible that observation carried out to inform assessment for accountability might damage ultimate achievement, since any valuable purpose it may have for future learning and development is a by-product that may be forgotten in the reporting of the outcome.

To an extent, an example of this in England is the *Foundation Stage Profile* (DfES, 2003), the assessment document completed by early years' practitioners for children reaching the end of that stage. Practitioners' professional judgements are founded on observations that take place before, and throughout, the child's time in the Foundation Stage and account is taken of dialogue with parents so that well-trained early years specialists use observations to inform planning for children to support their learning in the Foundation Stage. However, some practitioners have reported the Profile cumbersome and time-consuming to complete, taking them away from developing children's future learning and development. Additionally, it relates to the Foundation Stage's six areas of learning – only indirectly to the National Curriculum – and, perhaps because of this, some Year One teachers have reported finding it difficult to use as a starting point for children's learning in Key Stage One, particularly if they have little training in the early years. Despite the fact that the Profile is based on diagnostic assessments, it can therefore become a summative document that is not very useful in supporting children's future learning and development. Its purpose may well also be an attempt to establish value added to children's learning and development by the school, in order to ensure effective accountability at the cost of the provision of an 'ethical and safe environment in which all children learn' (Carr, 2001: 20).

The role of the practitioner in studying children effectively to preserve the integrity of children's learning and development becomes clearer. Respect for children and their families, materialized through dialogue and the promotion of children's agency in their learning and development as far as is possible, careful, varied observations carried out in a range of situations by expert practitioners and, finally, professional judgements arising from this sound, multiple perspective evidence base are all major tools in the early years' practitioner's workshop.

CASE STUDY

One September morning in the nursery, Sue, a senior practitioner, observes Devan, (3 years 1 month) for 30 minutes, noting every one of his actions and interactions. Among other activities, Devan stands near the sand tray, watching other children playing in the sand, moves to stand near another practitioner who is telling stories to a group of children and plays alone with a small red car, making it roll along a windowsill for several minutes. Sue does not interact with Devan during the time she is observing him, but after the children have gone home, Sue discusses what she observed with the practitioner team. The next day, she meets Devan's parents and shares what she observed. A plan emerges for the next stage of Devan's learning that is based on an holistic view of his achievements.

SUMMARY

The professional judgements that practitioners make about young children are interwoven with the knowledge and experiences of those practitioners. Highly skilled practitioners select and use methods and techniques judiciously and interweave their judgements with child and primary carer dialogues to inform planning for children's future development.

A greater holistic picture of the child and childhood appears to be perceived and constructed now more than ever before, through the combination of perspectives from different disciplines within integrated services, parent-partnership and an emerging picture of children's self-advocacy. The data – intended by policy and legislation to be used to support the child to fulfil his or her potential – contribute to the construction and perception of society now and in the future and attempt to ensure that public money is spent in line with policy and legislation. Intentions can be argued to be broadly altruistic for individuals and the larger population and have been devised by a democratically elected government.

However, while this has been happening, a view of childhood that begins with a destructive motive for the study of children has become more prevalent by being globally available. If we accept that views and realities of childhood might be a social construction, then we must accept that some views of childhood can also become a social destruction. What we see in some areas today could well develop into a more widespread reality tomorrow. The early years' practitioner can have a powerful role in greater construction, by putting the child's needs at the centre of child study.

QUESTIONS FOR REFLECTION AND DISCUSSION

1. How does what we see affect what we think?
2. How does what we think affect what we see?
3. What are the limitations of observations on children?
4. Whose perspective is normally left out of child studies and what are the implications of this approach?

Recommended reading

Bruce, T. and Meggitt, C. (2002) *Child Care and Education*. London: Hodder and Stoughton.

Carr, M. (2001) *Assessment in Early Childhood Settings: Learning Stories*. London: Sage.

Sharman, C., Cross, W. and Vennis, W. (1995) *Observing Children: A Practical Guide*. London: Continuum.

Chapter 9

International perspectives

Tim Waller

This chapter discusses a range of findings from recent international comparisons of early childhood education and care. A number of significant similarities and trends are identified, however, it is recognized that wider evidence is needed to represent a world view of early childhood education and care. The chapter provides an overview of early years policy and provision, commenting in more detail on diverse curricula and notions of 'quality'. Two examples of internationally renowned approaches to early years provision (Reggio Emilia in Italy and Te Whāriki from New Zealand) are briefly summarized to introduce students to the critical insights that can be developed through comparison. The chapter concludes with a consideration of the notion that 'children's services' should be replaced by 'children's spaces' (Moss and Petrie, 2002).

This chapter develops an overview of recent international comparisons of early years provision. Current issues and significant trends in early years care and education are identified and discussed. It is not the intention to provide detailed statistics, although some are given, rather to enable students of early childhood to engage in critical reflection on the benefit of cross-national studies.

Increasingly the UK is taking note of early years care and education policy and practice in other countries – notably those within Europe and the OECD (Organisation for Economic Co-operation and Development). This chapter explores the principles and practices adopted by a selected group of countries using the OECD thematic review as a framework. It aims to give students the opportunity to compare a variety of practices and consider possible outcomes and implications for children related to a holistic perspective. The chapter discusses both curricular and policy issues and encourages readers to critically analyse current policy and practice in early years care and education in the UK.

Recently the range of information and knowledge about international aspects of early years has increased due to the availability of online data and publications (see, for example, online early years journals such as *Contemporary Issues in Early Childhood* [*www.wwwords.co.uk/ciec*] and the *Journal of Early Childhood Research* [*ecr.sagepub.com*]). However, it should be acknowledged that most of the online material is available in English and to a large extent concerns English-speaking countries and Europe, so it does not represent a world view and a complete picture of early childhood education and care (see Waller et al., 2004). As Moss et al. (2003) point out, one of the problems of limiting our attention to those countries with which we are similar is that we risk missing some of the most important reasons for doing cross-national study. There is a need for wider comparison through further data from a greater number of countries around the world.

CONTEXT

A number of recent reports concerning early childhood education and care (ECEC) have identified some similarities and trends that allow broad international comparison. They also identify a diverse range of views of children, concepts of childhood and traditions and policies for ECEC adopted by the countries involved.

First the OECD provides a Thematic Review of Early Childhood Education and Care Policy [see *www.oecd.org*]. To date 18 countries have been reviewed: Australia, Belgium (two communities), Canada, Czech Republic, Denmark, Finland, France, Hungary, Ireland, Italy, Korea, Mexico, the Netherlands, Norway, Portugal, Sweden, United Kingdom, United States. Two countries remain to be reviewed in 2004: Austria and Germany. Bennett (2001) reported the following demographic, economic and social trends relevant to early childhood:

- Ageing populations, declining fertility rates, a greater proportion of children living in lone parent families
- A sharp rise in dual earner households, increased female employment rates

- Paid and job protected maternity and family leave seen as essential for parental support and equity but the level of payment and take-up varies across countries

- A significant increase in the number of refugee children and families from areas of conflict around the world – policy and attitude varies across countries.

Also, Moss et al. (2003) reported for the DFES on evidence from 15 countries, which were grouped according to differences in welfare regime. These included four 'English-language' countries (Australia, New Zealand, United Kingdom (UK) and the United States (USA)); four 'Nordic' countries (Denmark, Finland, Norway and Sweden) and seven 'Other European' countries (Belgium, France, Germany, Italy, the Netherlands, Portugal and Spain). The 15 countries were compared in terms of a number of demographic, employment, economic and policy dimensions, in relation to the welfare regime. Generally, there are strong similarities among the Nordic countries and among the English-language countries, with more variation among other European countries (paras. 5.1–5.7). The key findings of this study, which generally concur with Bennett (2001), include:

- Fertility rates are generally low (below replacement level except in the USA)

- The ageing of the European population

- English-language countries have high child poverty rates (defined as the proportion of children living in low income households) and the Nordic countries have low rates

- The US has the highest per capita national income, the highest child poverty and the lowest social expenditure and tax rates.

Moss et al. (2003: para. 5.5) also found that while women's employment is highest in the Nordic countries, part-time employment varies considerably. Employed women are most likely to work part-time in the Netherlands, Australia and the UK, and least likely to do so in Finland and Southern European countries. There are considerable variations in leave entitlements between different countries within the three groupings, in terms of length and payment. Including paid maternity and parental leave entitlements, Nordic countries offer the most generous leave arrangements to employed parents. While taken overall (and including levels of payment), the English-language countries offer the lowest levels of paid leave. The UK provides a longer period of paid leave than some countries in the 'other European' grouping – but most of the UK period of paid maternity leave is at a low flat-rate level, while Netherlands, Portugal and Spain pay an earnings-related benefit for their full maternity leave period.

The OECD report *Starting Strong* (Bennett, 2001) shows that the countries involved have adopted diverse strategies to ECEC policy and provision. These strategies are deeply embedded in particular contexts values, and beliefs. 'Early childhood policy and provision are strongly linked to cultural and social beliefs about young children, the role of the families and government and the purposes of ECEC' (OECD 2001: 38). For example, according to Anning and Edwards (1999: 13) the 'concepts of social responsibility and democratic decision making are high priorities in Danish cultural life'. In Denmark there is a tradition of providing funding for the integrated care of children, managed by local communities. Ofsted (2003) compared the education of six-year-olds in England, Denmark and Finland. They found that the curriculum is more centralized and prescribed in England and more importance is attached in Denmark and Finland to the way children develop as people. More is expected of English six-year-olds in terms of achievement in literacy and numeracy. In England children were also grouped according to 'ability'. These factors and differences relate to cultural values and the way each country views children.

POLICY AND PROVISION

Bennett (2003) argues that ECEC is increasingly viewed as a key component of national policy and that due to changes in economic conditions and child rearing patterns most countries were prepared to invest in ECEC to facilitate employment, promote children's cognitive, social and emotional development and life chances. The OECD (2001) report identifies the main focus of policy developments as:

● expanding provision to universal access
● raising the quality of provision

- promoting coherence and co-ordination of policy and services
- exploring strategies to ensure adequate investment in the system
- improving training and working conditions
- developing pedagogical frameworks for young children
- engaging parents, families and communities.

Within the OECD countries Bennett (2003) identified the following similarities and trends:

- most countries provide nursery education/kindergarten from three years
- considerable variation in provision for 0–3
- a persistent division between education and care.

Curtis and O'Hagan (2003: 201) point out that in Europe there is a general agreement on the division between policy and provision for children aged 0–3 and 3 to school age. However, the responsibility for the provision and the age of starting school varies (see Table 9.1). Curtis and O'Hagan also argue that Europe is 'united' in making inadequate provision for children from birth to three (e.g. poor training, poor salary levels, poor career structure, etc.), with the exception of Finland and Sweden. The UK National Childcare Strategy (2003) identifies three key problems with provision for children under three: the variable quality of provision; the high cost of childcare; the lack of provision in some areas. As Curtis and O'Hagan (2003) point out, legal entitlement to a place in childcare provision for children under three exists only in Sweden and Finland. In Sweden, from 18 months, and in Finland from birth. Both countries have excellent training provision for early childhood workers. Pascal and Bertram (2002) reported that few countries in the INCA survey had national curriculum guidelines for children under the age of three years. However, Pascal and Bertram argued that there was evidence of a general agreement that emphasis on individual children's developing interests and needs, dispositions and social and emotional well-being should be the focus of the curriculum for children under three years.

Table 9.1 Aspects of early years curricula across the study countries

Country	Organising body	Ages	Type of curricula
Nordic Countries			
Denmark	Municipal	0–6	No formal curriculum
Finland	National	0–6	All providers framework curriculum
Norway	National	0–6	All providers framework curriculum – children's culture, activities worked out by environment committee of parents/staff
Sweden	National	0–6	Publicly provided framework curriculum with democracy, citizenship, provision local interpretation environment, creativity (over 90 per cent of total). Welfare and education linked
English-speaking countries			
Australia	Territory	4–7	Public, private and expert driven (variation from territory to territory)
New Zealand	National	0–5	All licensed providers; Guidelines, local bicultural, bilingual not compulsory, i.e. in receipt of public interpretation broad inclusive of different funds principles and goals philosophies
UK (England)	National	3–6	Settings in receipt of expert, outcome-driven equal opportunities and government funding respect for diversity to provide early education
US	State	4–7	Variation from state range – from expert-driven; conflict between state to state to local interpretation curriculum and some national programmes

Table 9.1 *Continued*

Other countries

Belgium	Umbrella	3–6	All providers, expert-driven programme, Flanders and Walloon – each community has own programme
France	National	3–6	Public provision and expert-driven through 'livret scolaire'
Germany	Land	3–6	Public and voluntary basic principles only; local interpretation
Italy	Regional	3–6	Public provision; guidelines, 'oriamenti' citizenship, creativity only at national level
Netherlands	Municipal	4–6	Programme even; kindergarten not school, some private
Portugal	National	3–6	All jardins d'infancia; guidelines, not a programme; many Ministry of Education pedagogical models
Spain	National	0–6	All providers broad general framework; allowance made for initiatives at language and culture regional, local and e.g. Catalan. Pedagogical setting level principles for each curricular block

Source: Adapted from Moss et al., 2003: 8

Most European countries have both private and state provision for 0–3 and 3–5-year-olds. Curtis and O'Hagan argue that this diversity sometimes leads to a lack of co-ordination in services provided. In the UK, for example, despite the very welcomed adoption of the National Childcare Strategy in 1998, Moss and Petrie (2002: 172) suggest that policy and provision for young children has been characterized by a 'contract model' which has led to short-term funding requiring competitive bidding. The effect of this policy is to ensure central control through a standard approach (Gewirtz, 2000). Moss and Petrie discuss data from the Daycare Trust (2001) estimating that there were 45 different sources of funding for 'childcare services' in the UK. Scrivens (2002) distinguishes a tension between market driven policies and a new culture of professional inquiry; an inclusive view of education and care and a tighter outcomes-focused view of policy and practice.

Penn (1999) and Bennett (2003) identify the major policy challenges as: (i) the need to ensure sufficient public funding and adequate co-ordination of the agencies involved, and (ii) to improve the supply of services for children under three to meet the demand and to improve the recruitment training and remuneration of early years professionals (particularly for children under three).

Bennett (2001) and Penn (2003) acknowledge a range of common problems for the ECEC of children under three:

● local inequalities
● cash and funding
● fragmented and incoherent services
● responding to ethnic diversity.

CURRICULUM

Bennett (2003) shows that most OECD countries provide a curriculum framework for young children aged 3–6, but the frameworks differ greatly in terms of length, detail, prescription and pedagogical practice. Bertram and Pascal (2002) and Moss et al. (2003) also identify wide variations in how prescriptive the curricula are. Moss et al. found that leeway for local interpretation is common in the Nordic countries, and central specification strongest in England and France (paras 3.5–3.8). All curricula include general goals of personal development, language and communication. Bertram and Pascal (2002) found that there was some variation in how the ECEC curriculum for children over three was defined: most countries used areas of learning, few used activities, and no country used disciplines or subjects. Many countries emphasized cultural traditions and aimed to enhance social cohesiveness through the ECEC curriculum. Only three countries emphasized early literacy and numeracy within the ECEC curriculum. Moss et al. (2003) also found wide variation in terms of detail and benchmarking on specific subjects, skills and competencies (paras 3.5–3.8). They argued that each country in their report attempted to link curricula for early childhood services with entry to school in different ways. Only Sweden has a curriculum for out-of-school provision, though Finland, Spain, Sweden and France are developing curricula in this area (para. 3.12) (see Table 9.1).

The Qualifications and Curriculum Authority (QCA) in England commissioned an international review of the early years curriculum in 20 countries (Bertram and Pascal, 2002). The countries involved were Australia, Canada, France, Germany, Hong Kong, Hungary, Ireland, Italy, Japan, Korea, Netherlands New Zealand, Singapore, Spain, Sweden, Switzerland, UK England, UK N Ireland, UK Wales and the USA. Bertram and Pascal (2002: 7) identified the following five key areas of early childhood education and care as central to the debate:

1 The early years curriculum, viewed in its widest sense.
2 The issue of pedagogy (including staffing levels and the qualifications of staff).
3 The continuity of a child's experiences (within the setting, before arriving and after leaving the setting).
4 Definitions and measures of quality in early childhood settings.
5 Questions and key issues in the future development of early childhood education.

In their study Bertram and Pascal (2002: 8) argued that there was 'almost universal promotion of an active, play-based pedagogy within the participating countries, where self-management and independence were encouraged. Delegates generally agreed that the role of the adult was to support, scaffold and facilitate rather than to overly direct. Some countries, such as Sweden, specifically discouraged a formal approach.'

Bennett (2004), however, identified two different approaches to the curriculum for ECEC, for children over three years. First the 'social pedagogy' approach adopted by the Nordic countries and Central Europe. According to Bennett, the principle of this approach is a focus on the whole child involving a play-based, active and experiential pedagogy with an emphasis on the outdoors. A strong intergenerational and community outreach ethos is fostered. There is a short core curriculum to guide early education practice and local interpretation is encouraged. There is little systematic monitoring of child outcomes or measures, it is the centre's responsibility. Second the 'infant school' approach adopted by Australia, Belgium, France, Ireland, Korea, Mexico, Netherlands, UK (reception classes) and the USA. The focus of this approach is on 'readiness for school'. For Bennett, this approach is characterized by a restrained, teacher-directed play-based pedagogy where attention is given to achieving curricular aims and to measuring individual performance. There is central specification of a detailed curriculum and parental and community involvement is underplayed except in 'at risk' situations.

Despite the recent welcomed increased attention given to the ECEC of young children throughout many of the wealthier countries of the world, Bertram and Pascal (2002), Bennett (2003) and Moss et al. (2003) identify a number of barriers to development. Continuity in children's early experiences from home to setting and between settings is seen as a key to effective ECEC. The separation of education and care and early years and primary education, with different zones of ministerial responsibility, separate budgets and professional cultures is one of the most significant barriers. Further aspects of ECEC which need urgent attention are the status, training and career progression of staff and the gendered workforce.

The OECD (2001) report has signposted the way forward with the following 'Eight Key Policy Elements for Early Childhood Education and Care':

● a systemic and integrated approach to policy development and implementation
● a strong and equal partnership with the education system
● universal access and SEN
● substantial public investment
● a participatory approach to quality improvement and assurance
● appropriate training and working conditions
● systematic attention to data monitoring and collection
● a stable framework and long-term agenda for research and evaluation.

However, as Penn (2005) argues, while the OECD report provides useful comparative statistics and makes general recommendations, discussion is focused at the level of policy rather than practice. He makes the point that as with the EU, the OECD:

argues that equality of access and quality of practice are important goals for services, but that they can only be achieved by adequate public funding and by a good infrastructure of planning, evaluation and training. By these criteria the USA performs very poorly, almost bottom of the class. Nordic countries do very well. It is ironic that the US model, which stresses individual improvement at programme level, is so enthusiastically adopted by the World Bank and other international donors.

(Penn, 2005: 181)

QUALITY

While many countries have recently focused on expanding provision for young children, there has been at the same time a significant international trend to define and measure the effectiveness and 'quality' of that provision. The EU for example, developed 'A Framework for Quality for Early Childhood Services' (see Penn, 1999) stating that:

Equal access to good quality early years services is a goal of the European Union. Good quality services are a necessary part of the economic and social infrastructure. Equal access to these services is essential for equality of opportunity between men and women; for the well-being of children, families and communities; and for productive economies. It is a goal to be espoused at all levels – local, regional, national and European – and a goal for which all of these levels can and should work together.

(European Commission Network on Childcare and Other Measures to Reconcile Employment and Family Responsibilities, 1996)

First it is important to recognize that the need for definitions of quality come from a context of greater public accountability and expectations that services will provide 'value for money' (Elfer and Wedge, 1996) and the marketization of public services (Hill, 2003). Moss and Petrie (2002: 69) also discuss how the concept of 'quality' has been incorporated into ECEC from the commercial world. Second as (Pascal and Bertram, 1994: 3) point out, 'quality is value laden, subjective and dynamic'. 'Quality' is not universal but is a relative concept, depending on cultural values and beliefs about the nature of the children and childhood. Moss and Petrie recognize that in the field of early childhood 'quality' is increasingly discussed as a relative term with the possibility of multiple understandings and Raban et al. (2003) argue that acknowledging the complexity of measuring quality is actually desirable. (For a review of the debate about 'universal' or 'culturally specific' definitions of quality see Raban et al., 2003; and Dahlberg et al., 1999 for a more detailed discussion of quality).

As Penn (1999) points out, the notion of quality is meaningless unless there is clarity about values and beliefs that underpin a service. Elfer and Wedge (1996: 66) argue that 'quality is a misleading concept if it encourages the idea that we are all agreed on what we want for children before we have gone through a process to ensure that'. The difficulty is as Pence (1992) put it, who defines what is to be measured? Katz (1992) recognized three dimensions of quality: indicators, stakeholders, beneficiaries, and four perspectives: top-down, outside-inside, inside-out and bottom-up. Pascal and Bertram (1994) developed 10 dimensions of quality as part of their Effective Early Learning (EEL Project).

While there is recognition that a range of different interest groups such as children, parents, practitioners and stakeholders may all have different views of what quality means in terms of early childhood provision, there is an argument for developing common indicators of quality (Raban et al., 2003). Curtis and O'Hagan (2003: 169) discuss the guidelines for 'quality' early years provision that were developed by two international organizations, OMEP (the World Organisation for Early Childhood Education) and ACEI (American Childhood Education International) in 1999 [see *www.ecec21.org*]. These organizations agreed that effective early years provision involves 'a comprehensive network of services that provide:

- environment and physical space settings for children
- curriculum content and pedagogy
- early childhood educators and caregivers
- partnership with families and communities
- services for young children with special needs
- accountability, supervision and management of programmes for young children.

Within each area, special attention must be directed towards:

- services with equal attention to all children
- links between programmes and services
- recognition of the value of those who care for and teach young children including appropriate working conditions and remuneration
- intergenerational approaches whenever feasible
- empowerment of communities, families and children
- a mechanism for adequate and uninterrupted funding
- cost analysis, monitoring and evaluation of programme quality (Curtis and O'Hagan, 2003: 169–70).

Different ways of describing quality are defined as 'quality frameworks' such as the Early Childhood Environment Rating Scale [ECERS] (Harms et al., 1998). This framework has been used in the USA and the UK to evaluate the day-to-day functioning within settings (e.g. social interaction, children's activities, and physical facilities). These aspects are rated on a seven-point scale which is used as a diagnostic and longer-term monitoring tool. However, ECERS are generally used to provide a staff perspective and not that of children or parents. ECERS have also been used in research on early childhood (for example, Phillips et al., 1987; Sylva and Siraj-Blatchford, 2001). In particular, ECERS have provided data for the 'Effective Provision of Pre-school Education' (EPPE) project funded by the UK Department for Education and Skills on the developmental progress of more than 2,800 pre-school children in England [see *www.ioe.ac.uk/cdl/eppe/*].

'Quality' is a problematic concept and there is a real danger of focusing on a framework and on easily measurable standards such as space/size and not on qualitative aspects such as relationships and dispositions and the meanings constructed by those who use the setting. As Dahlberg et al. (1999) and Moss (2001d: 130) argue 'quality is not neutral it is socially constructed'. The concept of quality has created its own discourse ('Centres of Excellence', etc.) and evaluating the effectiveness of early years provision through predetermined, standardized criteria, according to Moss (2001d: 131), leads to 'a pedagogy of uniformity and normalisation ... and a definitive conclusion'. Dahlberg et al. (1999) and Moss (2001d) compare the 'discourse of quality' with an alternative 'discourse of meaning making' which 'recognises the negotiated and provisional nature of understanding and assessment' (Moss, 2001d:

132). The approach of the 'discourse of meaning making' therefore allows for judgements about the effectiveness of early years settings to be constructed, debated and disputed within a particular context based on data meaningful to the setting (for example, the use of pedagogical documentation in Reggio Emilia).

Two examples of internationally renowned early years provision are now discussed to encourage reflection and debate on international aspects of ECEC. For further details of the Reggio Emilia approach and Te Whāriki see *Five Curriculum Outlines*, OECD, 2004.

TE WHĀRIKI

Te Whāriki, the early childhood curriculum framework developed in New Zealand in 1996, has received a great deal of world-wide interest due to its innovative holistic and emergent approach to the curriculum. Whāriki (or mat) is used as a metaphor to signify the weaving together of the principles and strands as well as the diverse peoples, philosophies and services that participate in early education (Anning et al., 2004: 12). The view of the child is as 'a competent learner and communicator' and the approach fosters a holistic approach to curriculum planning and learning: 'The curriculum is founded on the following aspirations for children: to grow up as competent and confident learners and communicators, healthy in mind, body and spirit, secure in their sense of belonging and in the knowledge that they make a valued contribution to society' (MoE, 1996: 9).

According to Podmore (2004: 152), widespread consultation culminated in an innovative bicultural framework, with the document partly written in Maori. Te Whāriki received strong support from practitioners. The framework identifies learning outcomes for children as: working theories about the people, places and things in learner's lives and as learning dispositions (MoE, 1996). Te Whāriki invites practitioners to weave their own curriculum drawing on the framework of Principles, Strands and Goals. The focus is also on children's perspectives to define and evaluate (quality) practices in early childhood centres.

Te Whāriki has four central principles:

1 Empowerment.

2 Holistic development.

3 Family and community.

4 Relationships.

and five strands:

1 Well-being.

2 Belonging.

3 Contribution.

4 Communication.

5 Exploration.

The goals within each strand highlight ways in which practitioners support children, rather than skills or content, promoting a project-based approach drawing from the children's interests. Thus, the content emerges from children's interests which are tracked through the four principles. The guidelines apply to all children in all settings, including those with special educational needs who may be given an Individual Development Plan (IDP).

Local flexibility in content is seen as important to meet the needs of culturally diverse groups, including the Maori, within New Zealand. However, Anning et al. (2004: 12) argue that the strong free play tradition within ECEC in New Zealand has meant that practice has been slow to move away from individual self-selection of activities to collaborative learning through projects. Also, as with many other ECEC programmes across the world, despite the principles of Te Whāriki, Anning et al. identify a problem with top-down pressure from the government for more literacy and numeracy content within the curriculum. Cullen (1996) also argues that the flexibility of Te Whāriki can lead to early childhood programmes of variable quality.

Anning et al. (2004: 11) describe early childhood services in New Zealand 'primarily community based' with little shared history and few links between early childhood and primary education. However, since 2002 the New Zealand government has developed a 10-year strategic plan for early childhood (*Pathways to the Future: Nga Huarahi Aratiki*, MoE, 2002) with the aim to increase participation and quality of ECEC services and to promote collaborative relationships.

REGGIO EMILIA

Reggio Emilia has been internationally renowned for its early childhood programmes for over 40 years. Reggio Emilia is a city in the Emilia Romagna region of northern Italy with approximately 150,000 inhabitants. The region is one of the wealthiest parts of Europe. Since 1963, the municipality of Reggio Emilia has developed its own services for children from birth to six years of age, which have grown to include a network of 33 centres for young children. These are organized into *Asili Nido* (for children from three months to three years) and *Scuole del Infanzia* (3–6 years). The early childhood centres were established in close liaison with parents and the local community and children's rights are seen as paramount.

Loris Malaguzzi (1920–94) was the first head of municipal early childhood centres and significant influence on development of the Reggio approach. He advocated 'a pedagogy of relationships'. He held a positive and participatory view of early education and promoted a generous, optimistic view of human nature. For Moss (2001d), the significance of this positive approach is that it rejects the construction of the 'child at risk' or 'in need' not only because it produces a 'poor child', but also because it has chosen to move from the child as a subject of needs to a subject of rights.

Curtis and O'Hagan (2003: 217) summarise six principles of the Reggio Emilia approach as follows:

1 The study of child development as central to practice.
2 The importance of the teacher–child relationship.
3 The need for children's experiences to be taken into account when building the curriculum.
4 The importance of a rich environment in developing children's learning.
5 The importance of ongoing professional development for teachers.
6 The importance of the role of parents in the life of the school.

The main feature of the Reggio approach is that it advocates communication between adults and children and promotes collegiality and ethos of co-participation with families in the educational project (Nutbrown and Abbott, 2001: 1). Malaguzzi sees children as autonomously capable of making meaning from experience. 'Children's self-learning and co-learning are supported by interactive experiences constructed with the help of adults, who determine the selection and organisation of processes and strategies that are part of and coherent with the goals of early childhood education' (Malaguzzi, 1993: 78). As Rinaldi and Moss (2004: 2) point out in this approach 'learning is a process of constantly constructing, testing and reconstructing theories. Learning is a subject for constant research and must be made visible'. Knowledge is the product of a process of construction, involving interpretation and meaning making. It is co-constructed. Moss (2001d: 128) cites Rinaldi (a former pedagogical director of early years centres in Reggio) 'what children learn emerges from the process of self and social construction'. For Rinaldi 'learning is the subjective process of constructing reality with others'. The practitioner is therefore not a transmitter of knowledge and culture but facilitator in children's co-construction of their own knowledge and culture. The task of the practitioner is to offer a context in which the child can themselves explore and go deeper into a problem (Moss, 2001d: 129). Not only is the child viewed as a strong, powerful and competent learner, the child also has the right to an environment that is integral to the learning experience. Great value is placed on the whole environment as a motivating force:

> It is indisputable that schools should have the right to their own environment, their architecture, their own conceptualization and utilization of spaces, forms and functions. We place enormous value on the role of the environment as a motivating and animating force in creating spaces for relations, options and emotional and cognitive situations that produce a sense of well being and security.
>
> (Malaguzzi, 1996: 40)

As well as its commitment to developing 'deep, deep insight of children by listening to them', Nutbrown and Abbott (2001: 4) identify two further significant features of the Reggio approach. These are *time* (to discuss children and their projects) and *co-operative working* (teachers always work in pairs, each pair being responsible in the pre-schools for a group of children).

The Reggio approach is also characterized by a variety of pedagogical tools for developing early years practice in a rigorous, open and dynamic way. For example, pedagogical documentation, where learning processes are documented in various ways so that they can be shared, discussed, reflected upon and interpreted. Hoyuelos (2004: 7) suggests that this documentation represents an extraordinary tool for dialogue, exchange and sharing. It supports the ideological concept of the transparent school. For Vecchi (1993: 96), the procedure of documentation is a 'democratic possibility to inform the public of the contents of the school' and Rinaldi and Moss (2004: 3) argue that it is 'a unique source of information – precious for teachers, children, the family and anyone who wants to get closer to the strategies in children's ways of thinking'. For a more detailed discussion of pedagogical documentation see Dahlberg et al. (1999).

Reggio Emilia has become one of the best known early education systems in the world. Every year many early years specialists visit Reggio to study the approach and it has become so popular that since 1981 a Reggio exhibition 'The Hundred Languages of Children' has toured the world and there are 'Reggio networks' in 13 countries around the world (see Sightlines for details of the UK network). Reggio has been particularly influential in the USA and Sweden (see Dahlberg et al., 1999). Johnson (1999), however, argues that the widespread acclaim of Reggio Emilia has led to a 'cargo cultism' in early childhood education. He suggests that the Reggio Emilia approach has been 'Disneyfied', and colonized by the USA-dominated institutions and knowledge structures which have promoted it.

While there are clearly difficulties in attempting to replicate a system that developed in a particular (Italian) context and culture, the real significance of Reggio is that following visits to the region or the exhibition, many early years practitioners have been encouraged to critically reflect on and question their own practice (Moss, 2001b). As Curtis and O'Hagan (2003: 218) point out, 'adopting the approach means accepting and understanding the underlying principles and philosophy in the light of one's own culture'. Reggio has a lasting influence because, as Rinaldi and Moss (2004: 2) argue, 'Reggio is not a stable model producing predetermined and predictable outcomes, but a place where questions and uncertainty, change and innovation are welcome'. Moss (2001b: 125) reminds us that 'Reggio asks and expects us to ask many critical questions about ECEC. Reggio is so important because it reminds us that it is possible to think differently'. For Nutbrown and Abbott (2001) 'that capacity to provoke is perhaps one of the greatest and lasting legacies of any personal encounter with the Reggio Emilia experience'. As Gardner (2004: 16) asserts early childhood centres in Reggio 'stand as a shining testament to human possibilities'.

SUMMARY

This chapter has discussed a range of findings from recent international studies of early childhood education and care. A number of significant trends have been identified. Over the last 20 years or so, demographic, political and economic changes have led to significant interest and investment in ECEC. Bertram and Pascal (2002) argue that this 'new ECEC policy dynamic' is starting to make an impact throughout the world, which in some countries is 'revolutionary and unprecedented'. At the same time there is a tension between market driven policies and a new culture of professional inquiry. An inclusive view of education and care and a tighter outcomes-focused view of policy and practice (Scrivens, 2002). This is evident in approaches to the evaluation of ECEC and identification and measurement of 'quality'. The chapter discusses 'quality' as a problematic and culturally relative concept.

Two examples of internationally renowned approaches to early years provision (Reggio Emilia in Italy and Te Whãriki from New Zealand) are briefly summarized to introduce students to the critical insights that can be developed through comparison. As Bertram and Pascal (2002) and Moss et al. (2003) point out there are several benefits to cross-national studies. First by comparing provision in our own region or country with another we may question previously taken for granted traditional assumptions and practices. This process helps to make domestic practice visible and reveals the particular understandings of childhood, etc. that influence policy. It promotes critical thinking. For example, as Moss et al. (2003) point out, why is it that children in the UK start school earlier than almost everywhere else in Europe, and with what consequences? Why is education organized differently in different parts of the UK? There are, of course, limitations to the use of cross-national data and evidence. As Bertram and Pascal (2002) argue, policy and practice in ECEC is deeply located in national understandings of the place of family and childhood in society. The local context therefore needs to be taken into account and cross-national work needs to be interpreted. Given cultural norms, what is appropriate for one nation may be totally unsuitable for another. Differences in language and meaning can be problematic. For example, in the UK the term pre-school is taken to mean provision for children under five years, but in Sweden it is often used to describe the year before the start of formal schooling at seven years of age. The use of international statistics can also be problematic and is open to interpretation.

Moss (2001b) makes several important points regarding provision for young children. He argues that in a consideration of provision we should seek the views of the child. He argues that there are two possible constructions of early childhood institutions: as a place for the efficient production of predetermined outcomes, or as 'children's spaces' which provide opportunities for children and adults, the consequences of which may be unknown. The implication is that the term education and care is too restricting – care is not just about arrangements for working parents. He also suggests that a broader view of childhood is needed to take into account the relationships between the early childhood system and the education system. Further, Moss and Petrie (2002: 40) develop the model of seeking the views of children. They see children 'as young citizens and equal stakeholders with adults'. Moss and Petrie challenge early years practitioners and policy makers to reconceive provision for young children. They argue that as children have equal status and ownership of their environment the notion of 'children's services' should be replaced by 'children's spaces'. Dahlberg and Moss (2005) continue the debate by providing a strong argument for 'a narrative of possibilities' where early years practitioners are encouraged to be open to new thought and possibilities for ECEC (as in Reggio) and not tied down by 'a narrative of outcomes' which restricts early years practice to that which is measurable and predetermined.

QUESTIONS FOR REFLECTION AND DISCUSSION

1. What is the benefit of cross-national study?
2. What critical insights have you gained about ECEC provision in the UK as a result?
3. Do you have to visit a country to gain an understanding of ECEC in that country?
4. Why is measuring the 'quality' of ECEC always subjective?
5. What are the implications of early years practice in Reggio and New Zealand for early years settings in the UK?

Recommended reading

Anning et al. (2004) discuss early years provision and research in three different contexts: Australia, New Zealand and the UK.

Boushel (2000) reviews childrearing across a number of different cultures.

MacNaughton (2003) provides information on approaches to the early years curriculum from a range of countries across the world.

Moss and Petrie (2002) dedicate a whole chapter to ECEC in Sweden.

Penn (1997) compares nursery education and policy in Italy, Spain and the UK.

Penn (2000) presents an overview of global early childhood services.

Penn (2005) includes a chapter with a comparative overview of early years practice in China, North America, Europe and a number transitional countries such as Russia. She also briefly discusses practice and children's lives in a number of Asian and African countries and draws attention to studies such as Tobin (1995) who videoed life in nurseries in China, Japan and the USA.

The website *www.childcareincanada.org* is also a very useful source of international information about ECEC.

Bibliography

Abbott, L. and Hevey, D. (2001) 'Training to work in the early years: developing the climbing frame', in G. Pugh (ed.) *Contemporary Issues in the Early Years: Working Collaboratively with Children* (3rd edn). London: Sage.

Abrahams, C. (1994) *The Hidden Victims – Children and Domestic Violence*. London: NCH Action for Children. Available online at: *www.nch.org.uk* [Accessed 17/10/04].

Acheson, D. (1998) *Independent inquiry into inequalities in health*. Report of the committee chaired by Sir Donald Acheson. London: HMSO.

Alderson, P. (2005) 'Children's rights: a new approach to studying childhood', in H. Penn, *Understanding Early Childhood: Issues and Controversies*. Maidenhead: Open University Press and McGraw-Hill Education.

Alwin, D.F. (1990) 'Historical changes in parental orientations to children', *Sociological Studies of Child Development*, 3: 65–86.

Anning, A. and Edwards, A. (1999) *Promoting Children's Learning from Birth to Five*. Buckingham: Open University Press.

Anning, A., Cullen, J. and Fleer, M. (eds) (2004) *Early Childhood Education*. London: Sage.

Anning, A. (2004b) 'The co-construction of an early childhood curriculum', in A. Anning, J.Cullen and M. Fleer (eds) *Early Childhood Education*. London: Sage.

Aries, P. (1962) *Centuries of Childhood*. London: Cape.

Arnold, C. (2003) *Observing Harry: Child Development and Learning 0–5*. Maidenhead: Open University Press.

Athey, C. (1990) *Extending Thought in Young Children: A Parent–Teacher Partnership*. London: Paul Chapman.

Aubrey, C., David, T., Godfrey, R. and Thompson, L. (2002) *Early Childhood Educational Research*. London: Routledge Falmer.

Aubrey, C., Quick, S., Lambley, C. and Newcomb, E. (2002) *Implementing the Foundation Stage in Reception Classes*. London: Department for Education and Skills.

Bailey, R., Doherty, J. and Jago, R. (2003) 'Physical development and physical education', in J. Riley (ed.) *Learning in the Early Years: A Guide for Teachers of 3–7*. London: Paul Chapman Publishing.

Banks, S. (2004) *Ethics, Accountability and Social Professions*. Basingstoke: Palgrave Macmillan.

Bennett, J. (2001) 'Goals and curricula in early childhood', in S. Kammerman (ed.) *Early Childhood Education and Care: International Perspectives*. New York: The Institute for Child and Family Policy at Columbia University.

Bennett, J. (2003) 'Starting strong – the persistent division between education and care', *Journal of Early Childhood Research*, 1(1): 21–48.

Bennett, J. (2004) 'Curriculum Issues in National Policy Making'. Paper presented at the EECERA Annual Conference, Malta (September).

Bennett, N., Desforges, C., Cockburn, A. and Wilkinson, B. (1984) *The Quality of Pupils' Learning Experiences*. London: Lawrence Erlbaum.

Bennett, N., Wood, L. and Rogers, S. (1997) *Teaching Through Play: Teachers, Thinking and Classroom Practice*. Buckingham: Open University Press.

Berk, L. (2000) *Child Development* (5th edn). Boston: Allyn and Bacon.

Berk, L. and Winsler, A. (1995) *Scaffolding Children's Learning: Vygotsky and Early Childhood Education*. Washington DC: NAEYC.

Bertram, T. and Pascal, C. (2002) *Early Years Education: An International Perspective*. London: QCA/Nfer.

Bilton, H. (1999) *Outdoor Play in the Early Years: Management and Innovation*. London: David Fulton.

Blakemore, S.J. (2000) *Early Years Learning*. (Post Report 140) London: Parliamentary Office of Science and Technology.

Blakemore, S.J. and Frith, U. (2000) 'The implications of recent developments in neuroscience for research on teaching and learning'. ESRC-TLRP [available: *www.ex.ac.uk/ESRC-TLRP*].

Booth, T. and Ainscow, M. (eds) (1998) *From Them to Us: An International Study of Inclusion in Education*. London: Routledge.

Boushel, M. (2000) 'Child rearing across cultures', in M. Boushel, M. Fawcett and J. Selwyn (eds) *Focus on Early Childhood: Principles and Realities*. Oxford: Blackwell.

Blatchford, P. (1998) *Social Life in School*. London: Falmer Press.

BMA (2001) *Consents, Rights and Choices in Health Care for Children and Young People*. London: BMJ Books.

Bowlby, J. (1969) *Child Care and the Growth of Love*. Harmonsworth, Pelican.

Bransford, J.D., Brown, A.L. and Cocking R.R. (2000) *How People Learn: Brain, Mind, Experience and School*. Washington, DC: Academy Press.

Braye, S. (2000) 'Participation and involvement in social care: an overview', in H. Kemshall and R. Littlechild (eds) *User Involvement and Participation in Social Care: Research Informing Practice*. London: Jessica Kingsley Publishers Limited.

Bremner, G. and Fogel, A. (2004) *Infant Development*. Oxford: Blackwell.

Brierley, J. (1994) *Give me a Child Until he is Seven: Brain Studies and Early Education* (2nd edn). London: The Falmer Press.

British Educational Research Association Early Years Special Interest Group (BERA SIG) (2003) *Early Years Research: Pedagogy, Curriculum and Adult Roles, Training and Professionalism*. Southwell, Notts: BERA.

Bronfenbrenner, U. (1977) 'Toward an experimental ecology of human development', *American Psychologist*, 32: 513–531.

Brooker, E. (2002) *Starting School: Young Children Learning Cultures*. Buckingham: Open University Press.

Brooker, L. and Broadbent, L. (2003) 'Personal, social and emotional development: the child makes meaning in the world', in J. Riley (ed.) *Learning in the Early Years: A Guide for Teachers of 3–7*. London: Paul Chapman Publishing.

Brown, A. (1987) 'Metacognition, executive control, self-regulation and other more mysterious mechanisms', in F. E. Weinert and R. H. Kluwe (eds) *Metacognition, Motivation and Understanding*. Hillsdale, NJ: Erlbaum.

Brown, B. (1998) *Unlearning Discrimination in the Early Years*. Stoke on Trent: Trentham Books.

Bruce, T. (1991) *Time to Play in Early Childhood Education*. London: Hodder and Stoughton.

Bruce, T. (1996) *Helping Young Children to Play*. London: Hodder and Stoughton.

Bruce, T. (1997) *Early Childhood Education* (2nd edn). London: Hodder and Stoughton.

Bruce, T. (2001) *Learning Through Play – Babies, Toddlers and the Foundation Years*. London: Hodder and Stoughton.

Bruce, T. and Meggitt, C. (2002) *Child Care and Education*. London: Hodder and Stoughton.

Bruer, J.T. (1997) 'Education and the brain: a bridge too far', *Educational Researcher*, 26(8): 4–16.

Bruner, J.S. (1978) 'The role of dialogue in language acquisition', in A. Sinclair, R. Jarvella and W.J.M. Levelt (eds) *The Child's Conception of Language*. New York: Springer.

Bruner, J.S. (1986) *Actual Minds, Possible Worlds*. Cambridge, MA: Harvard University Press.

Bruner, J.S. (1990) *Acts of Meaning*. Cambridge, MA: Harvard University Press.

Bruner, J.S. (1996) *The Culture of Education*. Cambridge, MA: Harvard University Press.

Buckingham, D. (2000) *After the Death of Childhood. Growing Up in the Age of Electronic Media*. Cambridge: Polity Press.

Buckingham, D. (2004) 'New media, new childhoods? Children's changing cultural environment in the age of technology', in M.J. Kehily (ed.) *An Introduction to Childhood Studies*. Maidenhead: Open University Press and McGraw-Hill Education.

Burr, R. (2002) 'Global and local approaches to children's rights in Vietnam', *Childhood*, 9(1): 49–61.

Burr, R. (2004) 'Children's Rights. International policy and lived practice', in M.J. Kehily (ed.) *An Introduction to Childhood Studies*. Maidenhead: Open University Press.

Butcher, T. (2002) *Delivering Welfare* (2nd edn). Buckingham: Open University Press.

Calder, M.C. and Hackett. S. (eds) (2003) *Assessment in Child Care: Using and Developing Frameworks for Practice*. Lyme Regis: Russell House Publishing.

Canella, G.S. (1997) *Deconstructing Early Childhood Education: Social Justice and Revolution*. New York: Peter Lang.

Canella, G.S. and Greishaber, S. (2001) 'Identities and possibilities', in S. Greishaber and G. Canella (eds) *Embracing Identities in Early Childhood Education: 'Diversity and Possibilities'*. New York: Teachers College Press.

Carnwell, R. and Buchanan, J. (eds) (2005) *Effective Practice in Health and Social Care: A Partnership Approach*. Berkshire: Open University Press.

Carr, A. (ed.) (2000) *What Works With Children and Adolescents? A Critical Review of Research on Psychological Interventions with Children, Adolescents and their Families*. London: Routledge.

Carr, M. (2001) *Assessment in Early Childhood Settings*. London: Paul Chapman Publishing.

Carrier, J. and Kendell, A. (1995) 'Professionalism and inter-professionalism in health and community care: some theoretical issues', in Owens, P., Carrier, J. and Horder, J. (eds) *Inter-professional issues in community and primary health care*. London: Macmillan.

Caspi A., Newman D.L, Moffitt T.E. and Silva P. A. (1996) 'Behavioural observations at age 3 years predict adult psychiatric disorders' *Archives of General Psychiatry*, 53: 1033–1039.

Catherwood, D. (1999) 'New views on the young brain: offerings from developmental psychology to early childhood education', *Contemporary Issues in Early Childhood*, 1(1): 23–35.

Central Advisory Council for Education (1967) *Children and their Primary Schools* (the Plowden Report). London: HMSO.

Claxton, G. (1990) *Teaching to Learn*. London: Cassell.

Clark, A. and Moss, P. (2001). *Listening to Young Children: The Mosaic Approach*. London: National Children's Bureau.

Cohen, D., Stern, D. and Balaban, N. (1997) *Observing and Recording the Behaviour of Young Children*. New York: Teachers' College Press.

Cole, M. (1996) *Cultural Psychology: A Once and Future Discipline*. Cambridge, MA: The Belknap Press of Harvard University Press.

Connell, R. (1987) *Gender and Power*. Sydney: Allen and Unwin.

Corsaro, W.A. (1997) *The Sociology of Childhood*. London: Pine Forge Press.

Cousins, J. (1999) *Listening to Four-Year-Olds*. London: The National Early Years Network.

Cowley, S. and Houston, A. (2002) An empowerment approach to needs assessment in health visiting practice. *Journal of Clinical Nursing*, 11(5): 640–650.

Craig T. K. and Hodson. S. (1998) 'Homeless youth in London: I. childhood antecedents and psychiatric disorder', *Psychological Medicine*, 28(6): 1379–1388.

Crimmens, D. and West, A. (2004) *Having Their Say. Young People and Participation: European Experience*. Lyme Regis: Russell House Publishing.

CSIE (2000) *Index for Inclusion*. Bristol: Centre for Studies on Inclusion.

Cullen, J. (1996) 'The challenge of Te Whāriki for future development in early childhood education', *Delta*, 48(1): 113–25.

Cullen, J. (2004) 'Adults co-constructing professional knowledge', in A. Anning, J. Cullen and M. Fleer (eds) *Early Childhood Education*. London: Sage.

Cunningham, H. (1995) *Children and Childhood in Western Society Since 1500*. London: Longman Group Ltd.

Curry, N. and Johnson, C. (1990) *Beyond Self-esteem: Developing a Genuine Sense of Human Value*. Washington DC: NAEYC.

Curtis, A. (1994) 'Play in different cultures and different childhoods', in J.R. Moyles (ed.) *The Excellence of Play*. Buckingham: Open University Press.

Curtis, A. and O'Hagan, M. (2003) *Care and Education in Early Childhood*. London: Routledge.

David, T. (ed.) (1999) *Young Children Learning*. London: Paul Chapman Publishing Ltd.

Dahlberg, G. (1985) *Context and the Child's Orientation to Meaning: A Study of the Child's Way of Organising the Surrounding World in Relation to Public Institutionalised Socialisation*. Stockholm: Almqvist and Wiskell.

Dahlberg, G., Moss, P. and Pence, A. (1999) *Beyond Quality in Early Childhood Education and Care: Postmodern Perspectives*. London and New York: RoutledgeFalmer.

Dahlberg, G. and Moss, P. (2005) *Ethics and Politics in Early Childhood Education*. London and New York: RoutledgeFalmer.

De Mause, L. (ed.) (1976) *The History of Childhood*. London: Routledge.

Department for Constitutional Affairs (2004) *Freedom of Information Act (2004)*. Available online at: *http://www.dca.gov.uk* [Accessed 12/12/04].

Department for Education and Department of Health (1999) *National Healthy School Standards Document*. London: HMSO.

Department of Education and Science (1978) *Special Educational Needs: Report of the Committee of Enquiry into the Education of Handicapped Children and Young People*. London: HMSO.

Department for Education and Employment (1994) *Code of Practice on the Identification and Assessment of Special Educational Needs*. London: HMSO.

Department for Education and Employment (1997) *Excellence for All Children: Meeting Special Educational Needs*. London: HMSO.

Department for Education and Employment (1998) *The National Literacy Strategy*. London: Department for Education and Employment.

Department for Education and Employment (1999a) *The National Curriculum*. London: Department for Education and Employment and Qualifications and Assessment Authority.

Department for Education and Employment (1999b) *The National Numeracy Strategy*. London: Department for Education and Employment.

Department for Education and Employment (2000) *Curriculum Guidance for the Foundation Stage*. London: Qualifications and Curriculum Authority.

Department for Education and Skills (2001) *Special Educational Needs Code of Practice*. London: DfES Publications.

Department for Education and Skills (2001) *National Guidelines for Nutrition in Schools*. London: HMSO.

Department for Education and Skills and Qualifications and Curriculum Authority (2003) *Foundation Stage Profile*. London: Qualifications and Curriculum Authority.

Department for Education and Skills (2004a) *Meeting the Childcare Challenge*. Available online at: *www.standards.dfes.gov.uk* [Accessed 13/12/04.].

Department for Education and Skills (2004b) *Thinking Skills*. Available online at: *www.standards.dfes.gov.uk/thinkingskills/resources/565178? view=get – 24k –* [Accessed 12/12/04].

Department for Education and Skills (2004c) *Birth to Three Matters*. Available online at: *http://www.surestart.gov.uk* [Accessed 13/12/04].

Department of Education and Skills (2004d) *Children Act 2004*. London: HMSO.

Department of Education and Skills (2004e) *Every Child Matters: Change for Children*. London: HMSO. Available online at: *http://www.everychildmatters.gov.uk/* [Accessed 17/12/04].

Department of Health (1989) *Children Act 1989*. London: HMSO.

Department of Health (1991) *Working Together Under the Children Act 1989: A Guide for interagency Cooperation for the Protection of Children from Abuse*. London: HMSO.

Department of Health (1998) *Working Together to Safeguard Children: New Proposals For Interagency Cooperation*. London: HMSO. Available online at: *www.doh.gov.uk* [Accessed 17/12/04].

Department of Health (1998) *Saving Lives: Our Healthier Nation*. London: HMSO.

Department of Health (1999) *Making a difference: Strengthening the nursing, midwifery and health visiting contribution to health*. London: HMSO.

Department of Health (2000) *Framework for the Assessment of Children in Need and their Families*. London: HMSO.

Department of Health (2000) *The NHS Plan*. London: HMSO.

Department of Health (2001a) *School Nurse Practice Development Pack*. London: HMSO.

Department of Health (2001b) *Health Visitor Practice Development Pack*. London: HMSO.

Department of Health (2004) *National Service Framework for Children, Young People and Maternity services*. London: HMSO.

Department of Health (2004a) *Best Practice Guidance for Doctors and Other Health Professionals on the Provision of Advice and Treatment to Young People Under 16 on Contraception, Sexual and Reproductive Health*. Available online at: *http://www.dh./gov/uk/PublicationsAndStatistics/ PublicationsPolicyAnd Guidance/fs/en.* [Accessed 28/12/04].

Department of Health (2004b) *National Standards, Local Action: Health and Social Care Standards and Planning Framework*. London: Department of Health.

Department of Health (2004c) *National Service Framework for Children, Young People and Maternity Services: The Mental Health and Psychological Wellbeing of Children and Young People*. London: Department of Health.

Department of Health, Department for Education and Employment, Home Office (2004) *Framework for the Assessment of Children in Need and their Families*. London: The Stationery Office.

Department of Health and Social Security (1973) *Report on the Working Party on Collaboration Between the NHS and Local Government*. London: HMSO.

Diggle, L. (2004) Childhood Immunisation programme: current changes. *Community Practitioner*, 77(9) Sept: 347–349.

Dominelli, L. (2002) *Anti-oppresive Social Work Theory and Practice*. Basingstoke: Pallgrave Macmillan.

Donaldson, L., Mullally, S. and Smith, J. (2004) *New vaccinations for the childhood immunisation programme*. London: HMSO.

Donaldson, M. (1978) *Children's Minds*. Harmondsworth: Penguin.

Donaldson, M. (1992) *Human Minds: An Exploration*. Harmondsworth: Penguin Books.

Donaldson, M. (1993) 'Sense and sensibility: some thoughts on the teaching of literacy', in R. Beard (ed.) *Teaching Literacy Balancing Perspectives*. London: Hodder and Stoughton.

Doyle, C. (1997). 'Emotional abuse of children: issues for intervention', *Child Abuse Review*, 6: 330–342.

Draper, L. and Duffy, B. (2001) 'Working with parents', in G. Pugh (ed.) *Contemporary Issues in the Early Years*. London: Paul Chapman.

Drifte, C. (2001) *Special Needs in Early Years Settings: A guide for practitioners*. London: David Fulton.

Dunn, J. (1988) *The Beginnings of Social Understanding*. Oxford: Basil Blackwell.

Dunn, J., Bretherton, I. and Munn, P. (1987) 'Conversations about feeling states between mothers and their young children', *Developmental Psychology*, 23: 132–139.

Dweck, C. and Leggett, E. (1988) 'A social-cognitive approach to motivation and personality', *Psychological Review*, 95(2): 256–273.

Dwivedi, K. N. and Harper, B.P. (2004) *Promoting the Emotional Well Being of Children and Adolescents and Preventing Their Mental Ill Health: A Handbook*. London: Jessica Kingsley

Dyson, A. and Millward, A. (2000) *Schools and Special Needs: Issues of Innovation and Inclusion*. London: Paul Chapman.

Edgington, M. (2004) *The Foundation Stage Teacher in Action: Teaching 3, 4 and 5-Year Olds*. London: Paul Chapman.

Edwards, D. and Mercer, N. (1987) *Common Knowledge: The Development of Understanding in the Classroom*. London: Methuen.

Eekelaar, J. (1992) 'The importance of thinking that children have rights', in P. Alston and J. Seymour (eds) *Children's Rights and the Law*. Oxford: Clarendon Press.

Elfer, P. and Wedge, D. (1996) 'Defining, measuring and supporting quality', in G. Pugh (ed.) *Working Collaboratively for Children* (2nd edn). London: National Children's Bureau.

Eraut, M. (1999) 'Non-formal learning in the workplace'. Paper presented at Researching Work and Learning Conference, Leeds, September 1999.

Eyesearch.com. Available online at: *www.eyesearch.co,/optical.illusions.htm* [Accessed: 10/10/04].

Facer, K., Furlong, J., Furlong, R. and Sutherland, R. (2002) *ScreenPlay: Children and Computing in the Home*. London: RoutledgeFalmer.

Farson, R. (1974) *Birthrights*. London: Collier Macmillan.

Fawcett, M. (2000) 'Historical views of childhood', in M. Boushel, M. Fawcett and J. Selwyn (eds) *Focus on Early Childhood: Principles and Realities*. Oxford: Blackwell.

Finkelhor, D. (1984). *Child Sexual Abuse: New Theory and Research*. New York: The Free Press.

Fjørtoft, I. (2001) 'The natural environment as a playground for children: the impact of outdoor play activities in pre-primary school children', *Early Childhood Education Journal*, 29(2): 111–117.

Fjørtoft, I. and Sageie, J. (2000) 'The natural environment as a playground for children: landscape description and analyses of a natural playscape', *Landscape and Urban Planning*, 48: 83–97.

Fortin, J. (2003) *Children's Rights and the Developing Law*. London: Butterworth.

Franklin, B. (ed.) (2002) *The New Handbook of Children's Rights. Comparative Policy and Practice*. London: Routledge.

Freeman, M. (1983) *The Rights and Wrongs of Children*. London: Pinter.

Froebel, F. (1906) *The Education of Man*. New York: Appleton.

Frones, I. (1994) 'Dimensions of childhood', in J. Qvortrup, G. Sgritta and H. Wintersberger (eds) *Childhood Matters: Social Theory, Practice and Politics*. Aldershot: Avebury.

Gabriel, N. (2004) 'Being a child today', in J. Willan, R. Parker-Rees and J. Savage (eds) *Early Childhood Studies*. Exeter: Learning Matters.

Gardner, H. (1983) *Frames of Mind: The Theory of Multiple Intelligences*. New York: Basic Books.

Gardner, H. (2004) In, C. Rinaldi and P. Moss (2004) 'What is Reggio?', *Children in Europe*, (March), (6): 3.

Gerhardt, S. (2004) *Why Love Matters: How Affection Shapes a Baby's Brain*. Hove: Brunner-Routledge.

Gewirtz, S. (2000) 'Social justice, New Labour and school reform', in G. Lewis, S. Gewirtz and J. Clarke (eds) *Rethinking Social Policy*. London: Sage/Open University.

Gittins, D. (1998) *The Child in Question*. Basingstoke: MacMillan.

Gittins, D. (2004) 'The historical construction of childhood', in M.J. Kehily (ed.) *An Introduction to Childhood Studies*. Maidenhead: Open University Press and McGraw-Hill Education.

Gloucestershire Area Child Protection Committee (1995) *Part 8 Case Review Overview Report in Respect of Charmaine and Heather West*. Gloucester, Gloucestershire: GACPC.

Goldson, B. (2001) 'The demonization of children: from the symbolic to the institutional', in P. Foley, J. Roche and S. Tucker (eds), *Children in Society: Contemporary Theory, Policy and Practice*. Basingstoke: Palgrave.

Goldthorpe, L. (2004) 'Every child matters: a legal perspective, *Child Abuse Review*, 13: 115–136.

Gopnick, A., Meltzoff, A. and Kuhl, P. (1999) *How Babies Think: The Science of Childhood*. London: Weidenfield and Nicolson.

Gregory, E. (1996) *Making Sense of a New World: Learning to Read in a Second Language*. London: Paul Chapman Publishing.

Gregory, J., Lowe, S. and Bates, C.J. (2000) *National Diet and Nutrition Survey: young people aged 4 to 18 years*. Vol 1: Findings. London: HMSO.

Greeno, J. (1997) 'On claims that answer the wrong questions', *Educational Researcher*, 26(1): 5–17.

Hall, D. and Elliman, D. (2004) *Health for all Children* (4th edition). Oxford: Oxford University Press.

Hall, J. (1997) *Social Devaluation and Special Education*. London: Jessica Kingsley Publishers.

Hallet, C. (1995) 'Child abuse: an academic overview', in P. Kingston and B. Penhale (eds) *Family Violence and the Caring Professions*. London: Macmillan.

Hargreaves, L.M. and Hargreaves, D.J. (1997) 'Children's Development 3–7. The learning relationship in the early years', in N. Kitson and R. Merry (eds), *Teaching in the Primary School: A Learning Relationship*. London: Routledge.

Harms, T., Clifford, M. and Cryer, D. (1998) *Early Childhood Environment Rating Scale, Revised Edition (ECERS-R)*. New York: Teachers College Press.

Harrison, R., Mann G., Murphy, M., Taylor, T. and Thompson, N. (2003) *Partnership made Painless: A Joined Up Guide to Working Together*. Dorset: Russell House Publishing Ltd.

Hartup, W.W. (1996) 'The company they keep: friendships and their developmental significance', *Child Development*, 67: 1–13.

Hendrick, H. (1997) 'Constructions and reconstructions of British childhood: an interpretative survey, 1800 to the present', in A. James and A. Prout (eds) *Constructing and Reconstructing Childhood: Contemporary Issues in the Sociological Study of Childhood*. London: RoutledgeFalmer.

Henriques, J., Hollway, W., Urwin, C., Venn, C. and Walkerdine, V. (1984) *Changing the Subject: Psychology, Social Regulation and Subjectivity*. London and New York: Methuen.

Her Majesty's Government (1998) The Data Protection Act (1998). London: Her Majesty's Stationery Office.

Heppell, S. (2000) 'Foreword', in N. Gamble and N. Easingwood (eds), *ICT and Literacy*. London: Continuum.

Hetherington, E.M. and Parke, R.D. (1999) *Child Psychology*. Boston: McGraw Hill College.

Hill, D. (2003) 'Global neo-liberalism, the deformation of education and resistance', *Journal for Critical Education Policy Studies*, 1(1), March. Available online at: *http://www.jceps.com/?pageID=article&articleID=7* [Accessed 1/8/03].

Hill, M. (1999) 'What's the problem? Who can help? The perspectives of children and young people on their well-being and on helping professionals', *Journal of Social Work Practice*, 13(2): 17–21.

Hill, M. and Morton, P. (2003) Promoting children's interest in health: an evaluation of the child health profile. *Children and Society*, 17: 291–304.

Holland, P. (2004) *Picturing Childhood: The Myth of the Child in Popular Imagery*. London: I.B. Taurus.

Holt, J. (1974) *Escape From Childhood: The Needs and Rights of Childhood*. New York: EP Dutton and Co. Inc.

Hopkins, D. Ainscow, M. and West, W. (1994) *School Improvement in an Era of Change*. New York: Teachers College Press.

Housley, W. (2003) *Interaction in Multidisciplinary Teams*. Aldershot: Ashgate Publishing Limited.

Hoyles, M. and Evans, P. (1989) *The Politics of Childhood*. London: Journeyman Press.

Hoyuelos, A. (2004) 'A pedagogy of transgression', *Children in Europe* (March) (6): 6–7.

Hudson, J.A. (1993) 'Script knowledge', in M. Bennett, *The Child as Psychologist: An Introduction to the Development of Social Cognition*. New York: Harvester Wheatsheaf.

Hunter, M. (2004) *Hearts and Minds Reluctantly Follow as Bill Finally Completes Passage*. Available online at: *http//www.communitycare.co.uk/articles* [Accessed 16/01/05].

Huskins, J. (1998) *From Disaffection to Social Inclusion*. Bristol: John Huskins.

Hutt, C. (1966) 'Exploration and play in young children', *Symposia of the Zoological Society of London*, 18: 61–87.

James, A., James, A. (1999) 'Pump up the volume: listening to children in separation and divorce', *Childhood*, 6(2): 189–206.

James, A., James, A. and McNamee, S. (2004) 'Turn down the volume? not hearing children in family proceedings', *Child and Family Law Quarterly*, 16 (2): 189–202.

James, A., Jenks, C. and Prout, A.(1998) *Theorising Childhood*. Cambridge: Polity.

James, A. and Prout, A. (eds) (1997) *Constructing and Reconstructing Childhood: Contemporary Issues in the Sociological Study of Childhood*. London: RoutledgeFalmer.

Jarvis, J. and Lamb, S. (2000) 'Supporting children with communication difficulties', in R. Drury, L. Miller and R. Campbell (eds) *Looking at Early Years Education and Care*. London: David Fulton.

Jenkinson, J. (1997) *Mainstream or Special: Educating Students with Disabilities*. London: Routledge.

Jenks, C. (1982) *The Sociology of Childhood*. London: Batsford.

Jenks, C. (2004) 'Constructing childhood sociologically', in M.J. Kehily (ed.) *An Introduction to Childhood Studies*. Maidenhead: Open University Press.

Johnson, R. (1999) 'Colonialism and cargo cults in early childhood education: does Reggio Emilia really exist?', *Contemporary Issues in Early Childhood*, 1(1): 61–77.

Johnston, T. and Titman, P. (2004) A Health visitor led service for children with behavioural problems. *Community Practitioner*, 77(3) March: 90–94.

Jones, C. (2004) *Supporting Inclusion in the Early Years*. Maidenhead: Oxford University Press.

Jordan, B. (2004) 'Scaffolding learning and co-constructing understandings', in A. Anning, J. Cullen and M. Fleer (eds) *Early Childhood Education*. London: Sage.

Karstadt, L. and Medd, J. (2000) 'Promoting child health', in R. Drury, L. Miller and R. Campbell (eds) *Looking at Early Years Education and Care*. London: David Fulton.

Karstadt, L., Lilley, T. and Miller, L. (2000) 'Professional roles in early childhood', in R. Drury, L. Miller and R. Campbell (eds) *Looking at Early Years Education and Care*. London: David Fulton.

Kaltenborn, K. (2001) 'Family transitions and childhood agency', *Childhood*, 8(4): 463–498.

Katz, L.G. (1988) 'What should young children be doing?' *American Educator*, (Summer): 29–45.

Katz, L. (1992) *Five Perspectives on Quality in Early Childhood Program*, Perspectives from ERIC/EECE: A Monograph Series.

Katz, L.G. (1995) *Talks with Teachers of Young Children*. Norwood, NJ: Ablex.

Kehily, M.J. (ed.) (2004) *An Introduction to Childhood Studies*. Maidenhead: Open University Press and McGraw-Hill Education.

King, M. (1987) 'Playing the symbols – custody and the Law Commission', *Family Law*, (17): 186–191.

Labbo, L.D., Sprague, L., Montero, M.K. and Font, G. (2000) 'Connecting a computer center to themes, literature, and kindergartners' literacy needs', *Reading Online*, 4(1). Available online at: *http://www.readingonline.org/electronic/labbo/* [Accessed 6/8/00].

Laevers, F. (ed.) (1994) *The Leuven Involvement Scale for Young Children. Manual and Video. Experiential Education Series, No. 1.* Leuven, Belgium: Centre for Experiential Education.

Laevers, F. (2000) 'Forward to basics! Deep-level-learning and the experiential approach, in *Early Years*, 20(2): 19–29.

Laming, Lord (2003) *Inquiry into the death of Victoria Climbé*. London: The Stationery Office.

Lansdown, G. (2001) 'Children's welfare and children's rights', in P. Foley, J. Roche and S. Tucker (eds), *Children in Society, Contemporary Theory, Policy and Practice*. Basingstoke: Palgrave.

Lasenby, M. (1990) *Outdoor Play*. London: Harcourt Brace Jovanovich.

Lave, J. (1988) *Cognition in Practice*. Cambridge: Cambridge University Press.

Lave, J. and Wenger, E. (1991) *Situated Learning*. Cambridge: Cambridge University Press.

Leadbeater, C. (2004) *Learning about Personalisation: How Can we Put the Learner at the Heart of the Education System?* Annesley: Department for Education and Skills.

Leeson, C. and Griffiths, L. (2004) 'Working with colleagues', in J. Willan, R. Parker-Rees and J. Savage (eds) *Early Childhood Studies*. Exeter: Learning Matters.

Leiba, T. (2003) 'Mental health policies and inter-professional working', in J. Weinstein, C. Whittington and T. Leiba *Collaboration in Social Work Practice*. London: Jessica Kingsley Publishers.

Leiba, T. and Weinstein, J. (2003) 'Who are the participants in the collaborative process and what makes collaboration succeed or fail?', in J. Weinstein, C. Whittington and T. Leiba *Collaboration in Social Work Practice*. London: Jessica Kingsley Publishers.

Lepper, M. R., Drake, M. F. and O'Donnell-Johnson, T. (1997) 'Scaffolding techniques of expert human tutors', in M. Pressley and K. Hogan (eds) *Advances in Teaching and Learning*. New York: Brookline Press.

Lloyd, G., Stead, J. and Kendrick, A. (2001) *Interagency Working to Prevent School Exclusion*. York: Joseph Rowntree Foundation. Available online at: *http://www.jrf.org.uk/knowledge/findings/social* policy/961asp. [Accessed 10/10/04].

Lloyd-Smith, M. and Tarr, J. (2000) 'Researching children's perspectives: a sociological dimension', in A. Lewis, and G. Lindsay (eds), *Researching Children's Perspectives*. Buckingham: Open University Press.

Loxley, A. (1997) *Collaboration in Health and Welfare: Working with Difference*. London: Jessica Kingsley Publishers Limited.

Luke, C. (1999) 'What next? Toddler Netizens, playstation thumb, techno-literacies', *Contemporary Issues in Early Childhood*, 1(1): 95–100.

Macdonald, H., Henderson, R. and Oates, K. (2004) Low uptake of immunisation: contributing factors. *Community Practitioner*, 77(3) March: 95–100.

MacLeod-Brudenell, I. (ed.) (2004) *Advanced Early Years Care and Education*. Oxford: Heinemann.

MacNaughton, G. (2003) *Shaping Early Childhood*. Maidenhead: Open University Press.

MacNaughton, G. (2004) 'Exploring critical constructivist perspectives on children's learning', in A. Anning, J. Cullen and M. Fleer (eds) *Early Childhood Education*. London: Sage.

Malaguzzi, L. (1993) 'For an education based on relationships', *Young Children*, 11/93: 9–13.

Malaguzzi, L. (1996) 'The hundred languages of children', in Reggio Children, *The Hundred Languages of Children*. Reggio Emilia: Reggio Children.

Manning-Morton, J. and Thorp, M. (2003) *Key Times for Play: The First Three Years*. Maidenhead: Open University Press.

May, V. and Smart, C. (2004) 'Silence in court? Hearing children in residence and contact dipsutes', *Child and Family Law Quarterly*, 16 (3): 305–320.

Mayall, B. (ed.) (1994) *Children's Childhoods: Observed and Experienced*. London: Falmer Press.

Mayall, B. (1996) *Children, Health and the Social Order*. Buckingham: Open University Press.

Mayall, B. (2002) *Towards a Sociology of Childhood: Thinking From Children's Lives*. Buckingham: Open University Press.

Maynard, T. and Thomas, N. (eds) (2004) *An Introduction to Early Childhood Studies*. London: Sage.

Macormick, N. (1982) *Legal Rights and Social Democracy: Essays in Legal and Political Philosphy*. Oxford: Clarendon Press.

Merry, R. (1997) 'Cognitive development 7–11. The learning relationship in the junior years', in N. Kitson and R. Merry (eds), *Teaching in the Primary School: A Learning Relationship*. London: Routledge.

Meltzer, H., Gatward, R. and Goodman. R (2000) *Mental Health of Children and Adolescents in Great Britain*. London: Office of National Statistics.

Ministerial Group on The Family (1998) *Supporting Families: A consultation Document*. London: HMSO.

Ministry of Agriculture, Fisheries and Food (MAFF) (1997) *National Food Survey* London: HMSO.

Ministry of Education (1996) *Te Whariki: He Whaariki Matauranga: Early Childhood Curriculum*. Wellington: Learning Media.

Ministry of Education (2002) *Pathways to the Future: Nga Huarahi Aratiki. A 10-Year Strategic Plan for Early Childhood Education*. Wellington: Learning Media.

Monk, D. (2004) 'Childhood and the law: in whose best interests?', in M.J. Kehily (ed.) *An Introduction to Childhood Studies*. Maidenhead: Open University Press.

Mortimer, H. (2002) *Special Needs Handbook: Meeting Special Needs in Early Years Settings*. Leamington Spa: Scholastic.

Moss, P. (2001a) 'Britain in Europe: Fringe or heart?', in G. Pugh (ed.) *Contemporary Issues in the Early Years: Working Collaboratively for Children* (3rd edn). London: Paul Chapman Publishing.

Moss, P. (2001b) *Beyond Early Childhood Education and Care*. Report to OECD Conference, Stockholm 13–15 June.

Moss, P. (2001c) 'Policies and provisions, politics and ethics', in T. David (ed.) *Advances in Applied Early Childhood Education, Vol 1: Promoting Evidence Based Practice in Early Childhood Education*. London: JAI.

Moss, P. (2001d) 'The otherness of Reggio', in L. Abbott and C. Nutbrown (eds) *Experiencing Reggio Emilia: Implications for Preschool Provision*. Oxford: Oxford University Press.

Moss, P. and Pence, A. (1994) *Valuing Quality in Early Childhood Services*. London: Paul Chapman Publishing.

Moss, P. and Petrie, P. (2002) *From Children's Services to Children's Spaces*. London and New York: RoutlegdeFalmer.

Moss, P. and Petrie, P. (2003) *From Children's Services to Children's Spaces*. London: RoutledgeFalmer.

Moss, P., Petrie, P. and Poland, G. (1999) *Rethinking School – Some International Perspectives*. London: National Youth Agency. Available online at: *www.jrf.org.uk/knowledge/findings/social policy/n29.asp* [Accessed 5/11/03].

Moss, P., Candappa, M., Cameron, C., Mooney, A., McQuail, S. and Petrie, P. (2003) *Early Years and Childcare International Evidence Project: An Introduction to the Project*. London: DfES.

Moyles, J.R. (1989) *Just Playing? The Role and Status of Play in Early Childhood Education*. Buckingham: Open University Press.

Moyles, J.R. (ed.) (1994) *The Excellence of Play*. Buckingham: Open University Press.

Moyles, J.R. (1997) 'Just for fun? The child as an active learner and meaning maker', in N. Kitson and R. Merry (eds) *Teaching in the Primary School: A Learning Relationship*. London: Routledge.

Muller, P. (1973) 'Childhood's changing status over the centuries', in L.M. Brockman, J.H. Whiteley, and J.P. Zubak (eds) *Child development: Selected Readings*, 2–10. Toronto: McClelland and Stewart.

Murray, J. and Lumsden, E. (2004) 'Joining up the thinking – turning the policy into real practice'. Paper presented at the EECERA Annual Conference, Malta (September).

Mustard, F. and McCain, J. (1999) *Reversing the Real Brain Drain, Final Early Years Report for Ontario Government*. Ontario: Canada.

Norwich, B. (1997) *Inclusion or Exclusion: Future Policy for Emotional and Behavioural Difficulties Education. SEN Policy Options Steering Group*. Tamworth: NASEN.

Nutbrown, C. (ed.) (1996) *Children's Rights and Early Education*. London: Paul Chapman.

Nutbrown, C. (1999) *Threads of Thinking*. London: Paul Chapman.

Nutbrown, C. (2001) 'Watching and learning: The tools of assessment', in G. Pugh (ed.) *Contemporary Issues in the Early Years: Working Collaboratively for Children*. London: Paul Chapman.

Nutbrown, C. and Abbott, L. (2001) 'Experiencing Reggio Emilia', in L. Abbott and C. Nutbrown (eds) *Experiencing Reggio Emilia: Implications for Pre-school Provision*. Oxford: Oxford University Press.

Oberhuemer, P. and Ulich, M. (1997) *Working with Children in Europe*. London: Paul Chapman Publishing.

O'Brien, T. (ed.) (2001) *Enabling Inclusion: Blue Skies ... Dark Clouds?* London: Stationary Office.

OECD (2001) *Starting Strong – Policy Challenges for Early Childhood Education and Care Provision Across OECD Countries*. Paris: OECD.

OECD (2004) *Five Curriculum Outlines. Starting Strong: Curricula and Pedagogies in Early Childhood Education and Care*. Paris: OECD.

Office for Standards in Education (2003) *The Education of Six Year Olds in England, Denmark and Finland: An International Comparative Study.* London: Ofsted.

Office for Standards in Education (2004a) *NR 2004–126.* Available online at: *http://www.ofsted.gov.uk* [Accessed 12/12/04].

Office for Standards in Education (2004b) *The Future of Early Years Inspection.* Available online at: *http://www.ofsted.gov.uk* [Accessed 12/12/04].

Office for Standards in Education. (2004c) *The Future of Inspection: A Consultation Paper.* Available online at: *http://www.ofsted.gov.uk* [Accessed 12/12/04].

Parke, R. and Hertherington, E. (1999) *Child Psychology* (5th edn). Boston: McGraw Hill College.

Parry, A. and Jowett, S. (2001) The origins of early feeding problems. *Community Practitioner,* 74(4) April: 143–145.

Pascal, C. and Bertram, T. (eds) (1997) *Effective Early Learning.* London: Hodder and Stoughton.

Pascal, C. and Bertram, A.D. (1994) 'Defining and assessing quality in the education of children from 4–7 years', in F. Laevers (ed.) *Defining and Assessing the Quality in Early Childhood Education.* Studia Paedagogica (16). Leuven, Belgium: Leuven University Press.

Pascal, C., Bertram, A.D., Ramsden, F., Georgeson, J., Saunders, M. and Mould, C. (1996) *Evaluating and Developing Quality in Early Childhood Settings: A Professional Development Programme.* Worcester: Amber Publications.

Pea, R. D. (1993) 'Practices of distributed intelligence and designs for education', in G. Salomon (ed.) *Distributed Cognitions: Psychological and Educational Considerations.* Cambridge: Cambridge University Press.

Pence, A. (1992) 'Quality care: thoughts on R/rulers'. Paper presented at Workshop on Defining and Assessing Quality. Selville (September).

Penn, H. (1997) *Comparing Nurseries.* London: Paul Chapman.

Penn, H. (1999) *A Framework for Quality: A European Perspective.* London: Institute of Education, London University, May.

Penn, H. (ed.) (2000) *Early Childhood Services.* Buckingham: Open University Press.

Penn, H. (2005) *Understanding Early Childhood: Issues and Controversies.* Maidenhead: Open University Press and McGraw-Hill Education.

Phillips, D., McCartney, K. and Scarr, S. (1987) 'Child care quality and children's social development', *Journal of Applied Developmental Psychology,* 23(4): 537–543.

Pinkerton, J. (2001) 'Developing Partnership Practice', in P. Foley, P.J. Roche and S. Tucker (eds) *Children in Society: Contemporary Theory, Policy and Practice.* Basingstoke: Palgrave.

Podmore, V.N. (2004) 'Questioning evaluation quality in early childhood', in A. Anning, J. Cullen and M. Fleer (eds) *Early Childhood Education*. London: Sage.

Pollard, A. (1996) *The Social World of Children's Learning: Case Studies of Pupils from Four to Seven*. London: Cassell.

Pollard, A. (2000) 'Child agency and primary schooling', in M. Boushel, M. Fawcett and J. Selwyn (eds) *Focus on Early Childhood: Principles and Realities*. Oxford: Blackwell.

Pollock, L. (1983) *Forgotten Children – Parent: Child Relations from 1500–1900*. Cambridge: Cambridge University Press.

Postman, N. (1983) *The Disappearance of Childhood*. New York: W.H. Allen.

Powell, A. (2004) 'High court challenge to secret abortions for under-16s', *Daily Mail*, 15 December: 33.

Public Health Institute of Scotland (2003) *Need Assessment Report on Child and Adolescent Mental Health*. NHS: Scotland.

Pugh, G. (ed.) (2001) *Contemporary Issues in the Early Years: Working Collaboratively with Children* (3rd edn). London: Sage.

Qvortrup, J., Bardy, M., Sgritta, G. and Wintersberger, H. (eds) (1994) *Childhood Matters: Social Theory, Practice and Politics*. Aldershot: Avebury.

Raban, B., Ure, C. and Manjula, W. (2003) 'Multiple perspectives: acknowledging the virtue of complexity in measuring quality', *Early Years*, 23 (1): 67–77.

Radford, M. (1999) 'Co-constructing reality: the child's understanding of the world', in T. David (ed.) *Young Children Learning*. London: Paul Chapman Publishing Ltd.

Reder, P., Duncan, S. and Gray, M. (1993) *Beyond Blame: Child Abuse Tragedies Revisited*. London: Routledge.

Rickinson, M., Dillon, J., Teamey, K., Young Choi, M., Morris, M. and Benefield, P. (2003) *A Review of Research on Outdoor Learning: Summary of Interim Findings*. Reading: NFER.

Rigby, K. (2002) *New perspectives on bullying*. Jessica Kingsley, London.

Riley, J., (ed.) (2003) *Learning in the Early Years: A Guide for Teachers of 3–7*. London: Paul Chapman Publishing.

Rinaldi, C. and Moss, P. (2004) 'What is Reggio?' *Children in Europe*, (March) (6): 2–3.

Robbins, H. (2004) Minor illness education for parents of young children. *Journal of Advanced Nursing*, 44(3): 238–247.

Roberts, R. (1998) 'Thinking about me and them', in I. Siraj-Blatchford (ed.) *A Curriculum Development Handbook for Early Childhood Educators*. Stoke on Trent: Trentham Books.

Roberts, R. (2002) *Self-esteem and Early Learning*. London: Paul Chapman Publishing.

Robson, C. (1993) *Real World Research*. Oxford: Basil Blackwell.

Roche, J. (2001) 'Social work values and the law', in L. Cull and J. Roche (eds) *The Law and Social Work*. Basingstoke: Palgrave.

Roffey, S. (2001) *Special Needs in the Early Years*. London: David Fulton.

Rofrano, F. (2000) 'A response to colonialism and cargo cults in early childhood education: does Reggio Emilia really exist?', *Contemporary Issues in Early Childhood*, 1(2): 227–230.

Rogoff, B. (1990) *Apprenticeship in Thinking: Cognitive Development in Social Context*. New York: Plenum Press.

Rogoff, B. (1997) 'Evaluating development in the process of participation: theory, methods and practice building on each other', in E. Amsel and K.A. Renninger (eds) *Change and Development: Issues of Theory, Method and Application*. Mahwah, NJ and London: Erlbaum.

Rogoff, B. (1998) 'Cognition as a collaborative process', in D. Kuhn and R.S. Seigler (eds), *Handbook of Child Psychology*, Vol 2, (5th edn). New York: John Wiley.

Rogoff, B. (2003) *The Cultural Nature of Human Development*. New York: Oxford University Press.

Rose, S. (1989) *From Brains to Consciousness? Essays on the New Sciences of the Mind*. London: Penguin.

Ryder, M. and Wilson, B. (1997) 'From center to periphery: shifting agency in complex technical learning environments', Paper presented at the American Educational Research Association, Chicago, March.

Sainsbury, C. (2000) *Martian in the Playground, Understanding the Schoolchild with Asperger's Syndrome*. Bristol: Lucky Duck Publishing.

Saljo, R. (1999) 'Learning as the use of tools: a sociocultural perspective on the human-technology link', in K. Littleton and P. Light (eds) *Learning with Computers*. London: Routledge.

Salomon, G. (ed.) (1993) *Distributed Cognitions: Psychological and Educational Considerations*. Cambridge, UK: Cambridge University Press.

Sanders, B. (2004) 'Interagency and multidisciplinary working', in T. Maynard and N. Thomas (eds) *An Introduction to Early Childhood Studies*. London: Sage Publications.

Sayeed, Z. and Guerin, E. (2000) *Early Years Play: A Happy Medium for Assessment and Intervention*. London: David Foulton.

Schaffer, H.R. (1992) 'Joint involvement episodes as contexts for cognitive development', in H. McCurk (ed.) *Childhood and Social Development: Contemporary Perspectives*. Hove: Lawrence Erlbaum.

Schaffer, H.R. (1996) *Social Development*. Oxford: Blackwell.

Schweinhart, L. (2001) 'How the High/Scope Perry preschool study has influenced public policy'. Paper given at Third International Interdisciplinary Evidence-based Policies and Indicator Systems conference, July 2001.

Schweinhart, L. J., Barnes, H. V., and Weikart, D. P. (1993) 'Significant benefits: the High/Scope perry preschool Study through age 27'. *Monographs of the High/Scope Educational Research Foundation*, 10. Ypsilanti, MI: High/Scope Press.

Scott, W. (1996) 'Choices in learning', in C. Nutbrown, *Respectful Educators – Capable Learners: Children's Rights and Early Education*. London: Paul Chapman.

Scott, W. (2001) 'Listening and learning', in L. Abbott and C. Nutbrown (eds) *Experiencing Reggio Emilia: Implications for Preschool Provision*. Buckingham: Open University Press.

Scrivens, C. (2002) 'Early childhood education in New Zealand: the interface between professionalism and the New Right', in L.K.S. Chan and E.J. Mellor (eds) *International Developments in Early Childhood Services*. New York: Peter Lang.

Selleck, D. and Griffin, S. (1996) 'Quality for the under threes', in G. Pugh (ed.) *Working Collaboratively for Children* (2nd edn). London: National Children's Bureau.

Sharland, M. (1997) cited in Diggle, L. (2004) Childhood immunisation programmes. *Community Practitioner*, 77(9) Sept: 347–349.

Shaw, I. (2000) 'Just inquiry? Research and evaluation for service users', in H. Kemshall and R. Littlechild (eds) *User Involvement and Participation in Social Care: Research Informing Practice*. London: Jessica Kingsley Publishers Limited.

Shuttleworth, D. (2003) *School Management in Transition*. London: Routledge Falmer.

Silin, J. (1995) *Sex, Death and the Education of Children: Our Passion for Ignorance in the Age of Aids*. New York: Teachers College Press.

Siraj-Blatchford, I. (2004) 'Quality teaching in the early years', in A. Anning, J. Cullen and M. Fleer (eds) *Early Childhood Education*. London: Sage.

Smidt, S. (2002) *A Guide to Early Years Practice*. London: RoutledgeFalmer.

Smith, P.K. (1978) 'A longitudinal study of social participation in pre-school children: solitary and parallel play re-examined', *Developmental Psychology*, 14: 517–523.

Smith P.K. and Cowie, H. (2003) *Understanding Children's Development*. Oxford: Blackwell.

Snodgrass-Godoy, A. (1999) 'Our right to be killed', *Childhood*, 6(4): 425–442.

Staggs, L. (2004) cited in S. Palmer (2004) 'Early years: the right start', *Times Educational* Supplement, 19 March, pp. 14–15.

Stainton-Rogers, W. (1989) 'The Social Construction of Childhood', in W. Stainton-Rogers, D. Harvey, J. Roche and E. Ask (eds) *Child Abuse and Neglect: Facing the Challenge*. London: Batsford.

Stainton-Rogers, W. (2001) 'Theories of Child Development', in P. Foley, J. Roche, and S. Tucker (eds) *Children in Society: Contemporary Theory, Policy and Practice*. Basingstoke: Palgrave.

Stainton-Rogers, W. (2004) 'Promoting better childhoods: constructions of child concern', in M.J. Kehily (ed.) *An Introduction to Childhood Studies*. Maidenhead: Open University Press and McGraw-Hill Education.

Stakes, R. and Hornby, G. (1997) *Meeting Special Needs in Mainstream Schools*. London: David Fulton.

Steedman, C. (1990) *Childhood, Culture and Class in Britain, Margaret McMillan 1860–1931*. London: Virago.

Stone, C.A. (1998) 'What is missing in the metaphor of scaffolding?', in D. Faulkener, K. Littleton and M. Woodhead (eds) *Learning Relationships in the Classroom*. London: Routledge.

Sturge, C. and Glaser, D. (2000) 'Contact and domestic violence – the experts' court report', *Family Law*, (30): 615–629.

Sylva, K. (1994a) 'The impact of early learning on children's later development', in C. Ball (ed.) *Start Right: The Importance of Early Learning*. London: Royal Society of Arts.

Sylva, K. (1994b) 'School influences on children's development', *Journal of Child Psychology and Psychiatry*, 35(1): 135–170.

Sylva, K. (2003) *Assessing Quality in the Early Years*. Stoke on Trent: Trentham Publishers.

Sylva, K. and Siraj-Blatchford, I. (2001) 'The relationship between children's developmental progress in the pre-school period and two rating scales'. Paper presented at the International ECERS Network Workshop, Santiago, Chile (31 July).

Sylva, K., Melhuish, E. C., Sammons, P., Siraj-Blatchford, I. and Taggart, B. (2004) The Effective Provision of Pre-school Education (EPPE) Project: *Technical Paper 12 – The Final Report: Effective Pre-school Education*. London: DfES/Institute of Education, University of London.

Sylwester, R. (1995) *A Celebration of Neurones: An Educator's Guide to the Brain*. Alexandra, VA: ASCD.

Taylor, B. (1993) Childhood immunisation and family size. *Health Trends*, 25(1): 16–19.

Tharp, R. and Gallimore, R. (1991) 'A theory of teaching as assisted performance', in P. Light, S. Sheldon and M. Woodhead (eds) *Learning to Think*. London: Routledge.

The Editor (2001) 'Welcome to the tween age', *The Guardian*, 30 March, pp. 15.

Thomas, N. (2000) 'Listening to children', in P. Foley, J. Roche, and S. Tucker (eds) *Children in Society: Contemporary Theory, Policy and Practice*. Basingstoke: Palgrave.

Thomas, N. (2004) 'Law relating to children', in T. Maynard and N. Thomas (ed.) *An Introduction to Early Childhood Studies*. London: Sage.

Thompson, N. (2003a) *Communication and Language: A Handbook of Theory and Practice*. Basingstoke: Palgrave.

Thompson, T. (2003b) 'Learning disabilities: effective partnership and teamwork to overcome barriers in service provision', in J. Weinstein, C. Whittington and T. Leiba (eds) *Collaboration in Social Work Practice*. London: Jessica Kingsley Publishers.

Thorpe, S. (2004) 'Positive engagement', *Care and Health*, 73: 22–23.

Tizard, B. and Hughes, M. (1984) *Young Children Learning*. London: Fontana.

Tobin, J. (1995) 'Post-structural research in early childhood education', in J. Hatch (ed.) *Qualitative Research in Early Childhood Settings*. Connecticut: Praeger.

Tomlinson, S. (1982) *A Sociology of Special Education*. London: R.K.P.

Trevarthen, C. (1977) 'Descriptive analyses of infant communicative behaviour', in H.R. Schaffer (ed.) *Studies in Mother–Infant Interaction*. London: Academic Press.

Trevarthen, C. (1993) 'The functions of emotions in early infant communication and development', in, J. Nadel and L. Camaiori (eds) *New Perspectives on Early Communicative Development*. London: Routledge.

United Nations Educational, Scientific and Cultural Organisation (1989) *Convention on the Rights of the Child*. Paris: United Nations Educational, Scientific and Cultural Organisation.

United Nations Educational, Scientific and Cultural Organisation Almaty Office (2004) *Six Education For All Goals*. Available online at: *http://www.unesco.kz/index.php?lang=&sector=Education&newsid=854* [Accessed 2/8/04].

UNICEF (2004) *The State of the World's Children*. New York: UNICEF.

United Nations Children's Fund (2003) *The Best Start in Life for Every Child*. Available online at: *www.unicef.org/earlychildhood/* [Accessed 24/7/04].

Vecchi, V. (1993) 'Role of the atelierista', in C. Edwards, L. Gandini and G. Foreman (eds) *The Hundred Languages of Children – The Reggio Emilia Approach to Early Childhood Education*. Norwood, NJ: Ablex.

Velleman, R. and Templeton, L. (2003) 'Alcohol, drugs and the family: results from a long running research programme within the UK', *European Addiction Research*, 9: 103–112.

Vygotsky, L.S. (1978) *Mind in Society*. Cambridge, MA: Harvard University Press.

Vygotsky, L.S. (1986) *Thought and Language*. New York: MIT Press.

Walkerdine, V. (1984) 'Developmental psychology and the child-centred pedagogy', in J. Henriques, W. Hollway, C. Urwin, C. Venn and V. Walkerdine (eds) *Changing the Subject: Psychology, Social Regulation and Subjectivity*. London and New York: Methuen.

Walkerdine, V. (1993) 'Beyond developmentalism', *Theory & Psychology*, 3(4): 451–469.

Walkerdine, V. (2004) 'Developmental psychology and the study of childhood', in M.J. Kehily (ed.) *An Introduction to Childhood Studies*. Maidenhead: Open University Press and McGraw-Hill Education.

Waller, T., Murray, J. and Waller, J. (2004) 'Outdoor learning and well being: children's spaces and children's minds'. Paper presented at the EECERA Annual Conference, Malta 1–4 September 2004.

Webb, E. (2001) 'The health of children in refuges for women victims of domestic violence: cross-sectional descriptive study', *BMJ*, 323: 210–213

Weinstein, J., Whittington, C. and Leiba, T. (2003) *Collaboration in Social Work Practice*. London: Jessica Kingsley Publishers.

Wells, G. (1987) *The Meaning Makers*. London: Hodder and Stoughton.

Wenger, E. (1998) *Communities of Practice: Learning, Meaning and Identity*. Cambridge: Cambridge University Press.

Wertsch, J.V. (1985) *Culture, Communication and Cognition*. Cambridge, UK: Cambridge University Press.

Whalley, M. (2001) 'Working as a team', in G. Pugh (ed.) *Contemporary Issues in the Early Years: Working Collaboratively with Children* (3rd edn). London: Sage.

White, J. (2003) Barriers to eating 'five a day' fruit and vegetables. *Community Practitioner*, 76(10) October: 377–380.

Whittington, C. (2003) 'Collaboration and partnership in context', in J. Weinstein, C. Whittington and T. Leiba, *Collaboration in Social Work Practice*. London: Jessica Kingsley Publishers.

Willan, J., Parker-Rees, R. and Savage, J. (2004) *Early Childhood Studies*. Exeter: Learning Matters.

Willey, C. (2000) 'Working with parents in early years settings', in R. Drury, L. Miller and R. Campbell (eds) *Looking at Early Years' Education and Care*. London: David Fulton.

Willow, C., Marchant, R., Kirby, P. and Neale, B. (2004) *Young Children's Citizenship*. York: Joseph Rowntree Foundation.

Wilson, R. (1998) *Special Educational Needs in the Early Years*. London: Routledge.

Wilson, T. (2000) Factors influencing the immunisation status of children in a rural setting. *Journal of Paediatric Health Care*, 14: 117–121.

Wolfendale, S. (2000) 'Special needs in the early years: prospects for policy and practice', *Support for Learning*, 15 (4).

Wood, E. and Attfield, J. (1996) *Play, Learning and the Early Years Curriculum*. London: Paul Chapman.

Wood, D.J., Bruner, J.S., and Ross, G. (1976) 'The role of tutoring in problem solving', *Journal of Child Psychology and Psychiatry*, 17(2): 89–100.

Woodhead, M. (1999) 'Towards a global paradigm for research into early childhood education', *European Early Childhood Research Journal*, 7(1): 5–22.

Woodhead, M. (2003) 'Childhood studies: past, present and future'. Paper presented at Open University Conference, 'Childhood Reconsidered', 27 June.

Wells, G. (1987) *The Meaning Makers*. London: Hodder and Stoughton.

World Health Organisation (1999) *A Critical Link – Interventions for Physical Growth and Psychological Development*. World Health Organisation.

Wray, D. and Medwell, J. (1998) *Teaching English in Primary Schools*. London: Letts.

Wright, S. (2000) 'Why Reggio Emilia doesn't exist: a response to Richard Johnson', *Contemporary Issues in Early Childhood*, 1(2): 223–226.

Yelland, N.J. (1999) 'Technology as play', *Early Childhood Education Journal*, 26(4): 217–225.

Young Minds (2003) *Tuning in to Our Babies: The Importance of the Relationship Between Parents and Their Babies and Toddlers*. London: Young Minds.

Zelitzer, V. (1985) *Pricing the Priceless Child*. New York: Basic Books.

Zuckerman, M. (1993) 'History and developmental psychology: a dangerous liaison', in G. Elder, J. Modell and R. Parke (eds) *Children in Time and Space: Developmental and Historical Insights*. Hillsdale, NJ: Lawrence Erlbaum Associates.

Index

Added to the page number 'f' denotes a figure and 't' denotes a table.

A

abortion, young peoples' rights 9
abuse xv
  children's reactions 20–2
  contexts 15–16
  definitions 14
  disclosure 23
  recognition *see* recognition of abuse
accessibility 32
accommodation 89
accountability 115, 116, 119–20, 133
The Acheson Report 74
adaptation, processes of 89
adults
  role in the social construction of childhood
    61–3
  see also parents
age of criminal responsibility 2
'Age of Enlightenment' 85
agency 63, 109–10, 116
  and education practitioners 121
  and health care practitioners 117
  and social care practitioners 118
  see also self-advocacy
anxiety disorders 81
'Apgar Score' 116
appearance and recognition of abuse 22
assessment 114, 116, 120
  purposes 106–7
  see also school league tables; *The National
    Assessment Framework*
Assessment Framework of Children in Need
    and their Families 41
assimilation 89
associative play 99

attention deficit 81
autistic spectrum 32

B

babies
  screening 116
  symptoms of mental illness 81
balance of power see power balance
behaviour and recognition of abuse 22
behaviourism 87
bias in professional judgements 111
Birth to Three Matters 114, 119
brain development 66–8
bruising 17
Bruner, J. S. 89

C

'C' (codified) knowledge 111
Centre for Studies on Inclusive Education
    (CSIE) 30
chaotic context for abuse 15–16
'the' child
  definition 2, 61
  see also 'normal' child; 'rich child'
child development 3, 11, 56–8, 59
  criticisms of the central role of xiii, xvi
  and ecological systems theory 65
  effect of early experience 67
  influence of behaviourism 87
  and recognition of abuse 23
  significance of play 99
  socio-cultural or 'situative perspective' 66, 91
child health xvi, 70–83
  role of health visitors see health visitors
  role of primary health care
    practitioners 72–3
    case study 73
  role of school nurses *see* school nurses
  working with families 74

child health promotion 76–82
  immunization 76–7
  mental illness *see* mental illness
  nutrition 77–8
    case study 78
  physical activity 78–9
child liberationists 3
childhood vaccinations
  schedule 77t
  uptake 76–7
children
  and the co-construction of their own
    childhood 61–5, 114
  'conditions of power' impacting on 65
  early interactions between parents and 93–4
  impact of digital technology on 61
  listening to 64, 109
  participation in family, community and
    culture 65–6
  protection of *see* protection of children
  seeking the views of 142
  study of *see* study of children
  views on their success as learners 91
  see also Vietnamese street children
Children Act (1989) 7, 39, 41, 46, 64
Children Act (2004) xiii, 7–8, 39, 40, 46
Children [Scotland] Act (1996) 7
children's centres xiii
Children's Commissioner 7–8
children's rights xv
  definition 1–2
  see also participation rights; protection rights
'children's spaces', replacement of 'children's
    services' with 142
clients *see* service users
Climbé, Victoria 13, 41
co-construction 93
  of their own childhood by children 61–5, 114
co-operative play 99
Code of Practice for Special Educational
    Needs (1994 and 2001) 29
collaboration *see* professional collaboration
collaborative play 99
communication
  and collaboration 48–9
  see also interagency communication
community development initiatives 72
competence 3, 8–11, 64
  and the Children Act (1989) 7
  and the United Nations Convention on the
    Rights of the Child (UNCRC) (1989) 5

concrete operational stage 88
'conditions of power' 65
construction of childhood *see* social construction
    of childhood
constructivism 87–9
contact decisions and children's rights to
    participation 9–11
corrupting behaviour 20
criminal responsibility, age of 2
'critical periods' for learning 67
cross-national studies, benefits 141–2
CSIE (Centre for Studies on Inclusive
    Education) 30
Curriculum 2000 29
curriculum frameworks
  international perspective 130–3
  see also early years curricula; National
    Curriculum
Curriculum Guidance for the Foundation Stage
    114, 119

D
data and child study 112, 121–2
'deep level learning' 97
degrading behaviour 20
degrees in early childhood studies xiii, 50, 52–3
destruction of childhood 113, 115, 122
development of children *see* child development
developmental psychology 56–7, 58, 59, 68, 86
deviant context for abuse 16
dialogue 108–9, 116
  and education practitioners 121
  and health care practitioners 117
  and social care practitioners 118
digital technology, impact on children's lives 61
disability, models of 31–3
Disability Movement 32
disclosure of abuse 23
'discourse of meaning making', comparison of
    'discourse of quality' with 135–6
dispositions *see* learning dispositions
disruptive behaviour disorders 81
diverse childhoods, multiple and 56–9
diversity, recognition of 14–15
domains for child study 112–13

E
early brain development 66–8, 102
early childhood education and care (ECEC),
    international perspectives *see*
    international perspectives

Early Childhood Environment Rating Scale (ECERS) 135
early childhood institutions, constructions 142
early childhood studies degrees xiii, 50, 52–3
early intervention 30, 72
Early Years Action 29
Early Years Action Plus 29
early years curricula
  centrality of play 102
  international perspective 127–9, 131
  see also Reggio Emilia; Te Whāriki
Early Years Development and Childcare Partnerships (EYDCP) 31
Early Years Sure Start Endorsed Foundation Degrees 52–3
eating disorders 81
ECEC (early childhood education and care), international perspectives *see* international perspectives
ECERS (Early Childhood Environment Rating Scale) 135
ECHRC (European Convention on Human Rights) 2
ecological systems theory 65
Education Act (1944) 28
Education Act (1981) 28, 108
education and children's rights to participation 9
education practitioners and child study 119–21
  case study 121
'Effective Provision of Pre-school Education' (EPPE) project 135
'Eight Key Policy Elements for Early Childhood Education and Care' 132
elimination disorders 81
embedded learning 88
emotional abuse
  definition 14
  understanding and recognizing 19–20
employment of women 125
enactive representation 89
Epistemic play 99, 100f
EPPE (Effective Provision of Pre-school Education) project 135
equity 56
'essential childhood' 56
European Convention on Human Rights (ECHRC) 2
Every Child Matters: Change for Children xvi, 39, 40, 42, 49, 53, 71
Excellence for all Children 31

Excellence in Schools 31
EYDCP (Early Years Development and Childcare Partnerships) 31

F
failure to thrive, non-organic 17
families
  and health care and preventative work 72, 74
  see also parents
family health plans 74
family proceedings and children's rights to participation 9–11
fantasy play 99, 101, 102
fear inducing behaviour 19
feeding disorders 81
formal operations 88
Foundation Stage Profile 120
'A Framework for Quality for Early Childhood Services' 133
Freud, S. 101
friendship, influence on learning 95
Froebel, F. 101
frozen fright 21
fruit and vegetables, intake of 78

G
Games with Rules 99, 100f
Gardner, H. 89–90
Gesell, A. 86
Gillick v West Norfolk and Wisbech Area Health Authority (1985) 8–9
grading 120
'grooming' 19
growth retardation 17
Guatemalan street children 6

H
health of children *see* child health
health practitioners
  child study by 116–17
  see also primary health care practitioners
health screening 116–17
health visitors 72, 73, 74
  and nutrition 78
healthy schools 76
'helpless' learning dispositions 91
'hot-housing' 67
human rights 2
  inclusion as 30–1

I
iconic representation 89
IEPs (Individual Education Plans) 29
imbalance of power *see* power balance
immunization 76–7
inappropriate roles 20
inclusion xv–xvi, 27–38
  aspects of good practice 37
  case studies 34–7
  definition 30
  global and national perspective 29–30
  hindrances 33
  as a human right 30–1
  legislative framework 28–9
  models of disability and the role of special
    schools 31–3
'infant school' approach to the curriculum
    131–2
'Instrumentality (thinking, rationality and
    logic)' 111
inter-subjectivity 92–3, 94
interagency collaboration *see* professional
    collaboration
interagency communication 43t
interagency working 43t
international literature and research, overview
    xvi, 55–69
international perspectives xvii, 123-42
  context 124–6
  curriculum 130–3
  policy and provision 126–30
    challenges 130
  quality of provision 133–6, 141
  Reggio Emilia 138–41
  Te Whãriki 136–7
interprofessional working, distinction between
    multiprofessional and 44–5
involvement, signs of 97–8
Isaacs, S. 101
isolating behaviour 20

J
joined-up 43t
'joint involvement episodes' 94
joint working 43t

L
language, learning 84
language of collaboration 42–6, 48
  overcoming the barriers of 48–9
league tables 33, 64, 114

learning xvi, 84–104
  'critical periods' 67
  effect on the structure of the brain 68
  modern ideas 87–98
    constructivism 87–9
    learning as a relationship and a disposition
      93–8
    metacognition 90–1
    multiple intelligence 89–90
    scaffolding 92–3
    social constructivism 91–2
  outdoor 103
  play and *see* play
  in the Reggio Emilia approach 139
  traditional ideas 85–7
learning dispositions 91, 94, 96–8
  domains 98
'learning stories' 98
leave entitlement 125–6
listening to children 64, 109
  see also seeking the views of children model
Locke, J. 86
Ludic play 99, 100

M
Making a Difference 72, 74
Malaguzzi, L. 138–9
'mastery' learning dispositions 91
maturationist view of learning 86–7
medical model of disability 31–2
mental illness 79–82
  common classifications 81-2
  manifestations 80–1
  resilience to 80
  susceptibility to 80
  treatment approaches 82
metacognition 90–1
mission statements 49
mistreatment *see* abuse
MMR vaccine 77
modern theory of childhood 55–69
  children's participation in family, community
    and culture 65–6
  co-construction by children of their own
    childhood 61–5, 114
  multiple and diverse childhoods 56–9
  multiple perspectives of childhood 59–61
  new areas of knowledge and understanding
    66–8
'Mongolian blue-spot' 17
Montessori, M. 101

'motherese' 94
multiagency working 43t
multiple and diverse childhoods 56–9
multiple intelligence 89–90
multiple perspectives of childhood 59–61
multiprofessional working 43t
   distinction between interprofessional and
      44–5
mutuality 92

N
'narrative of outcomes' 142
'narrative of possibilities' 142
The National Assessment Framework 118
National Childcare Strategy xiii, 113–14, 127
National Curriculum 114
National Health School Standard (NHSS) 75
   and nutrition 78
   recommendation for physical activity 78
National Literacy Strategy 114
National Numeracy Strategy 114
National Service Framework for Children,
      Young People and Maternity Services 71
National Service Frameworks (NSF) Primary
      Care Trusts 75
neglect
   definition 14
   understanding and recognizing 17
neuroscientific research 66–8, 102
new sociology of childhood 57, 58, 59–60
NHS Plan (2000) 74
non-organic failure to thrive 17
'normal' child 56–7
nutrition 77–8
   case study 78

O
obesity 77
   reducing the risk 79
observation 107–8, 112–13, 116
   by education practitioners 119, 120, 121
   by health practitioners 117
   by social care practitioners 118
online data and publications 124
outdoor learning 103

P
'P' (personal) knowledge 111
parallel play 99
parents
   dialogue with 109

early interactions between children and 93–4
   priorities 64
   and the promotion of child health 82
   as service users 64
participation rights 1–12
   and the Children Act (1989 and 2004) 7–8
   and competence *see* competence
   conflict between protection rights and 3–4
   and the United Nations Convention on the
      Rights of the Child (UNCRC) (1989)
      4–6
partnerships
   characteristics of successful 43–4
   definition 42–3
   start of 51
Pathways to the Future: Nga Huarahi Aratiki 137
pedagogical documentation 139–40
performance related indicators 33, 64
pervasive development disorders 81
physical abuse
   definition 14
   understanding and recognizing 17
physical activity
   health benefits 79
   promotion of 78–9
Piaget, J. 87–9
   and play 101
plasticity 67
play 98–102
   categories 99–100
   outdoor 103
   purpose 100–2
   stages 99
power balance
   between adults and children 62, 63, 65, 113
   and service user involvement 48
pre-operational period 88
pretend play 99, 102
primary health care practitioners 72–3
   case study 73
   see also health visitors; school nurses
Primary National Strategy 114
Primary Schools/Primary Care Health Links
      Project 75
professional collaboration xvi, 39–54
   difficulties 45
   ingredients for successful 50–1
   language of *see* language of collaboration
   in practice 46–9
   and the role of training in early years 51–3
professional judgements 115, 116
   making 110–11, 121

professional workers' attitudes to abuse 23
protection of children xv, 13–26
    and the Children Act (2004) 7
    and recognizing diversity 14–15
protection right 1
    conflict between participation rights and xv,
        3–4, 11
    in the United Nations Convention on the
        Rights of the Child (UNCRC) (1989) 5
provision rights 5
psychological contrast 21–2

Q
'quality frameworks' 135
quality of provision 133–6, 141

R
reactions to abuse, understanding and
        recognizing 20–2
recognition of abuse 13–14, 22–5
    case study 24–5
    emotional abuse 19–20
    obstacles to 23–4
    physical abuse 17
    sexual abuse 17–19
    and workers' attitudes 23
Reggio Emilia 138–41
rejecting behaviour 20
relationships and learning 93–8, 109
residence disputes and children's rights to
        participation 9–11
'rich child', concept of 63
rights
    definition 1–2
    see also children's rights; human rights
rights-based perspective, criticism 4
rigid context for abuse 16
Rogoff, B. 91–2, 93
role play 100, 101
Romantic view of learning 85–6
Rousseau, J. J. 85

S
Salamanca statement 29
Saving Lives: Our Healthier Nation 72, 74
scaffolding 92–3
schemas 87
school league tables 33, 64, 114
school nurses 72, 74–6
    case study 75

and nutrition 78
screening 116–17
seeking the views of children model 142
    see also listening to children
segregated model of disability 32–3
self-advocacy 110, 114, 121
    see also agency
self-concept 95, 96
self-esteem 12, 95–6
sensori-motor stage 88
separation anxiety disorder 81
service users 64
    working in collaboration with 46–9
sex offenders 18–19
sexual abuse
    definition 14
    understanding and recognizing 17–19
sexual matters, young peoples' rights to
        confidentiality 9
single agency working 43t
'situative perspective' on child development 66
social care practitioners and child study
        118–19
    case study 119
social construction of childhood 2, 58
    legislation and 2
    role of adults 61–3
    and the study of children 113–14, 122
social constructivism 91–2, 102
social destruction of childhood 113, 115, 122
social inclusion 33
social model of disablement 32
'social pedagogy' approach to the curriculum 131
socio-cultural perspective on child
        development 66, 91
sociology of childhood 57, 58, 59–60
solitary play 99
Special Educational Needs and Disability Act
        (2001) 32
Special Educational Needs (SEN), inclusive
        practice see inclusion
special schools, role 31–3
Starting Strong 126
statements and recognition of abuse 23
Stockholm syndrome xv, 21–2
study of children xvii, 106–22
    agency see agency
    by education practitioners 119–21
        case study 121
    by health practitioners 116–17
        case study 117

by social care practitioners 118–19
  case study 119
construction of childhood and 113–14
dialogue *see* dialogue
domains 112–13
making professional judgements 110–11
observation *see* observation
purposes 106–7
reasons for 115–16
study of early childhood xiii
  see also training
subjectivity 111
successful learners, characteristics 104
Supporting Families 74
Sure Start programmes xiii, 30, 72
  see also Early Years Sure Start Endorsed
    Foundation Degree
'surveillance' 116
sustained shared thinking 94
symbolic representation 89

T
Te Whāriki 136–7
'teenage' culture 61
'Ten Bedrock Principles' 107
testing 120
Thematic Review of Early Childhood
    Education and Care Policy (OECD)
    124–5
tic disorders 82
tormenting behaviour 20
Tourettes disorder 82
'traffic light' card system 49
training, role in early years xvi, 51–3
'transformation of participation' 93
'tweenagers'/'tweenies' 61

U
UK National Childcare Strategy xiii, 113–14,
    127
unconditional acceptance 96
unexceptional context for abuse 15
United Nations Convention on the Rights of
    the Child (UNCRC) (1989) 2, 4–6, 46,
    110, 113
United Nations Educational, Scientific and
    Cultural Organisation (UNESCO)
    Salamanca statement 29

V
vaccinations *see* childhood vaccinations
vegetables, intake of fruit and 78
Victoria Climbé 13, 41
Vietnamese street children 2, 6
Vygotsky, L.
  and play 101–2
  and the 'zone of proximal development'
    (ZPD) 92, 115

W
Warnock Report (1978) 28
welfare regimes, differences in 125–6
well-being 97, 98
women's employment 125
workers' attitudes to abuse 23
Working Together Under the Children Act
    39-40

Z
'zone of proximal development' (ZPD) 92,
    115